D0090952

AN INTERVIEW
WITH GOD

AN INTERVIEW WITH GOD

Questions You're Asking and How the Bible Answers Them

Woodrow Kroll

MOODY PUBLISHERS
CHICAGO

© 2004 by
WOODROW KROLL

All rights reserved. No part of this book may be reproduced in any form without permission in writing from the publisher, except in the case of brief quotations embodied in critical articles or reviews.

All Scripture quotations, unless otherwise indicated, are taken from the *Holy Bible, New International Version*®. NIV®. Copyright © 1973, 1978, 1984 by International Bible Society. Used by permission of Zondervan Publishing House. All rights reserved.

Scripture quotations marked KJV are from the King James Version.

Scripture quotations marked NKJV are taken from the *New King James Version*. Copyright © 1982, 1992 by Thomas Nelson, Inc. Used by permission. All rights reserved.

Scripture quotations marked NLT are taken from the *Holy Bible, New Living Translation*, copyright © 1996. Used by permission of Tyndale House Publishers, Inc., Wheaton, Illinois 60189. All rights reserved.

Scripture quotations marked THE MESSAGE are from *The Message*, copyright © by Eugene H. Peterson 1993, 1994, 1995. Used by permission of NavPress Publishing Group.

Scripture quotations marked CEV are taken from the *Contemporary English Version*. Copyright © 1991, 1992, 1995 by American Bible Society. Used by permission.

The use of selected references from various versions of the Bible in this publication does not necessarily imply publisher endorsement of the versions in their entirety.

Library of Congress Cataloging-in-Publication Data

Kroll, Woodrow Michael, 1944-
An interview with God : questions you're asking and how the Bible answers them / by Woodrow Kroll ; foreword by George Barna.
p. cm.
ISBN 0-8024-1622-5
1. Bible—Miscellanea. I. Title.

BS612.K76 2004
231.7—dc22

2003026385

1 3 5 7 9 10 8 6 4 2

Printed in the United States of America

Dedicated to

All Honest Questioners

May you not just find answers;
May you find truth

Contents

Acknowledgments   9
Foreword   11
Preface   13

1. Questions God Will Answer (and some He won't) 15
2. Appreciating God's Answers   21

GOD'S ANSWERS TO YOUR QUESTIONS
3. Predictions   29
4. Life Purpose   41
5. Life After Death   57
6. Problems in the World   71
7. Suffering   93
8. About My Life   103
9. Personal Request   115
10. Faith & Spirituality   129
11. Miscellaneous   141

Author's Epilogue   153
Appendix: How the Barna Poll Was Conducted 157

Acknowledgments

I want to thank George Barna, founder and president of Barna Research Group, from whose creative mind the idea for this book was born. My appreciation to Lynn Gravel, project director for Barna Research Group, and to those who worked diligently to find out the questions that Americans wanted to ask God, tabulating them, and analyzing the subsequent data. Thanks to Cameron Hubiak of Barna Research for his valuable assistance.

I am grateful to Moody Publishers for publishing this book. This team has been amazing and the commitment and involvement of so many people is gratifying. Special thanks to Mark Tobey, Director of Acquisitions, with whom I have worked so closely, and General Editor Ali Childers.

And a great deal of appreciation must be expressed for my own team here at Back to the Bible. Thanks to Cathy Strate, who has worked with me for more than two decades providing assistance in proofreading, editing, and substantiating biblical reference, and to Allen Bean, my research and editorial assistant. You both have worked tirelessly and without complaining to bring good things to life.

And to my family, especially my wife, Linda. Thank you for your support, your continuous prayers during long hours of research and writing, and for your love. Without you, my writing would find much less purpose.

Finally, thanks to all those who participated in the poll conducted by Barna Research Group. Without your questions, the rest of us would have had no reason to respond. God bless you all.

Foreword

More than nine out of every ten Americans believe that God exists. Although a huge majority of adults say they have established a comfortable peace with God, deeper examination reveals most Americans are uneasy with the stability and serenity of that relationship. Thus it is not surprising that when we asked a national sample of adults if they would like to ask God a question, almost all of them jumped at the chance. (In fact, more than a few had a lengthy list of questions they wished to raise.) Who wouldn't want to get answers to tough questions directly from the source of truth and wisdom?

Not only did the 1,010 people we interviewed supply several hundred unique questions for God, but the range of those inquiries was also impressive. Some people were curious about their personal condition on earth, others wondered about their condition after their time on earth expires. Many focused on the reason for specific conditions in the world, others desired clarity regarding their purpose in life. More than a few of the questions were philosophical in nature, but most of them were personal and practical. You will recognize some questions as age-old stumpers, while a few may strike you as profound in their novelty and simplicity.

When I was growing up, my church discouraged me from asking such questions. That, in turn, dissuaded me from taking the Christian faith seriously. Fortunately, since then I have encountered people whose faith is strong enough to challenge God with their toughest questions and expect Him to respond. Most important, they have not come away disappointed. Following their example, I have embarked on a lifelong conversation with God, frequently asking questions and expecting answers. The result is that my own faith has flourished, for I have learned that there is no question too difficult or too sensitive for God to handle. You simply need the courage to ask Him, the faith to believe in His answers, and the knowledge of how to discern His answers.

Enter *An Interview With God*. Woodrow Kroll went right to the source of all truth and has provided us with a paraphrase of God's answers to each question. A lifelong student of God's words to humanity and a person devoted to maintaining an intimate relationship with God, Wood uses this book to teach us a magnificent theological lesson: God, in His inexhaustible wisdom, foresaw every one of your questions and has already provided you with timeless, practical, transcultural answers.

I pray that this book will fortify your confidence in God's wisdom, truth, and love. He always has the answer you need. As Jesus reminded us, we often do not have what we need because we do not ask for it. If you need God's wisdom, ask Him for it. And may *An Interview With God* help you to discern His voice.

George Barna
Ventura, California
December 2003

Preface

In every generation there is a certain amount of bewilderment as to why things are the way they are, what the future holds, and what our relationship to God is. These anxieties are reflected in the questions we ask God.

To learn what was on your mind, the Barna Research Group, Ltd., of Ventura, California, conducted a poll and asked American adults: "If you could ask God any question about your life, what is the single most important question you would want to ask Him?"

In previous polls asking a similar question, people responded with similar concerns. For example, *USA Today* asked, "If you could get in contact with God directly, ask a question, and get an immediate reply, what would you ask?" "What is my purpose here?" was the number one response (34 percent). The next was "Will I have life after death?" (19 percent), followed by "Why do bad things happen?" (16 percent). Other polls have yielded results similar to those of *USA Today.*[1] The questions that the Barna Research Group compiled tended to be more personal, less general and universal. That may be due to the fact that this poll was conducted during the winter of 2003 just prior to the war in Iraq.

Barna Research Group provided the question groupings. The questions themselves were provided by more than a thousand people. You will notice that the "God's Answer" sections use the first person voice of God. By using what God the Father has already said in His Word, the Bible, the answers reflect God's historic, written statements that speak to the questions raised. More than seven hundred Bible references are cited. However, this book is no substitute for reading the Word of God. The Bible is inspired by God and flawless. This is a gathering and interpretation of what God has already said, but it is *not* on the same level as the highest authority we've been given, the Bible. After years of Bible study and Bible teaching, I have searched for God's answers, but do not presume that the content of the following chapters is word-for-word from His mouth.

Perhaps you've been pondering a question that was asked by one of those polled. If your question was not asked, ask it yourself. God welcomes questions, and you'll find the answers in the pages of His Word.

Note

1. "Going to a Higher Authority," *USA Today,* 28 May 1999.

Questions God Will Answer (and some He won't)

While some people see the Bible merely as a book of rules, it is more accurately a book of questions. Literally thousands of questions are asked and answered within the pages of the Bible. Some of them are matters of life or death: "How shall we escape if we ignore such a great salvation?"[1] Some are far less profound: "Is there flavor in the white of an egg?"[2]

Should you be afraid to ask questions of God? Won't He zap you with a cosmic lightning bolt or something if you question Him? Doesn't the prophet remark, and the apostle repeat, that the creature is in no position to question the Creator?[3] But were Isaiah and Paul condemning our questioning nature? I don't think so. God made us inquisitive people. He gave us minds that want to know. We have a thirst to understand everything we can, even things that are beyond our grasp. That's good; it keeps us searching for truth when we encounter fabrication.

God is able to answer your questions. Some of the people closest to Him asked some of the toughest questions.[4] The secret is asking questions that God will answer. Let's identify what some of those questions are.

God answers questions that seek honest information.

Jesus was explaining to His disciples that He had to leave them in order to prepare a place for them and that they would follow Him. Thomas asked, "Lord, we don't know where you are going, so how can we know the way?"[5] Many times Thomas is called "doubting Thomas," and elsewhere he may deserve it, but not here. Did the disciples know what Jesus was talking about? Not entirely. Did they know the way? No. This was a legitimate question seeking honest information and Jesus did not rebuke Thomas. Instead He answered his question. (It was Philip whom Jesus rebuked in the next several verses for a lack of faith, not Thomas.) If you need answers, ask God.[6] It's legitimate to question God when you seek honest information.

God answers questions that seek clarification.

Nicodemus had heard Jesus' teachings, but he was puzzled. When Jesus said, "No one can see the kingdom of God unless he is born again," Nicodemus had a question. Jesus did not rebuke him for asking, "How can a man be born when he is old?"[7] This Jewish law expert and judiciary court (Sanhedrin) member wasn't being smart with the Savior; he simply didn't understand how a person could enter his mother's womb and be born a second time. His question sought clarification and Jesus answered him. You ought not be timid to ask God questions that seek explanation.

God answers questions that show sincerity.

Have you been part of a discussion group in which some of the questions were, well, just downright dumb? We all have. On the other hand, when Daniel was thrown into the lions' den, King Darius was genuinely interested in Daniel and went to the entrance of the den the next morning, asking, "Daniel, servant of the living God, has your God, whom you serve continually, been able to rescue you from the lions?"[8] That was a sincere request reflecting concern for a friend. God is more apt to provide answers to a sincere person who is really seeking Him.

God will most likely not answer questions with preconceived answers.

Sometimes we ask questions hoping God will confirm the answers we already have. In this case, we're not looking for omnipotent assistance; we're looking for a divine rubber stamp. There was a rich young man mentioned in the Bible who asked Jesus what he must do to inherit eternal life.[9] He had formulated a preconceived idea of what Jesus would say, so when Jesus answered differently than expected, the man was not prepared to accept His response. God is not inclined to answer questions that we have already answered in our minds and are just checking out God's opinion.

God will most likely not answer questions that are accusatory.

Have you ever shaken your fist in God's face and said something like, "God, why did You make me marry that guy? He's a loser and doesn't love me the way he's supposed to." Neither our choices nor sinful behavior is generated by God; it's generated by Satan. "For our struggle is not against flesh and blood, but against the rulers, against the authorities, against the powers of this dark world and against the spiritual forces of evil in the heavenly realms."[10] God doesn't answer questions that accuse Him of what He has not done. God may be the only Friend you have. If you want honest answers, don't accuse your Friend of what your enemy has done to you.

God will most likely not answer questions designed for entrapment.

Do you know the first question in the Bible? Satan asked Eve, "Did God really say, 'You must not eat from any tree in the garden'?"[11] The reason Satan asked the question was to trap Eve. She would have been better off to ignore that old snake. But often we ask God questions hoping to entrap Him. Wasn't that the intent of the Pharisees and Herodians when they asked Jesus, "Is it right to pay taxes to Caesar or not?"[12] Jesus didn't answer the question as they wanted because He knew their intent. He said, "You hypocrites, why are you trying to trap me?" How foolish it is to think we can question God and catch Him in our trap.

God will most likely not answer questions that are inherently illogical.

I would like to see the expression on God's face every time someone in a college philosophy class asks, "Can God make a rock so big He can't lift it?" God cannot do something that is a violation of His own nature. Said differently, God's morality will not permit Him to do something with His power that defies His intelligence or contradicts His character.

Satan tried that on Jesus but failed miserably. Each question in our Lord's temptation attempted to get Jesus to violate His nature and character of submission to His Father's will. (1) "If you are the Son of God, tell these stones to become bread," (2) "If you are the Son of God, throw yourself down [from the highest point of the temple]," and (3) "All [the kingdoms of the world] I will give you if you will bow down and worship me."[13]

By asking Jesus to do these things, Satan wanted Him to use His power to accomplish things that He was not ordained to do. If Jesus chose to, He could have left the wilderness and been at a table filled with food or have had the angels catch Him in the air after a jump from the temple. He could have abandoned His earthly mission to rule the world. But that was not the plan. Jesus did not need to do illogical things that would thwart His purpose as Servant and Savior to the world. His birthright, His deeds, and His teaching already proved His power and identity. And He will rule as King of Kings forever according to His Father's terms and timing.

God is not opposed to your questions. Quite the contrary.

He welcomes them. That's why there are so many questions asked and answered in the Bible. Come to Him with an open mind, read His Word with a searching heart, and leave your preconceived answers at home. You may be surprised what God will say to you.

Notes

1. Hebrews 2:3.

2. Job 6:6.

3. Isaiah 29:16; Romans 9:20.

4. Moses: "O LORD, why have you brought trouble upon this people?" (Exodus 5:22); Gideon: "If the LORD is with us, why has all this happened to us?" (Judges 6:13); Job: "Why have you made me your target? Have I become a burden to you?" (Job 7:20).

5. John 14:5.

6. James 1:5.

7. John 3:4.

8. Daniel 6:20.

9. Mark 10:17–31; Luke 18:18–30.

10. Ephesians 6:12.

11. Genesis 3:1.

12. Matthew 22:17–18.

13. Matthew 4:3, 6, 9.

Appreciating God's Answers

You are prepared to ask God your questions, but are you also prepared to appreciate His answers? When God answers your questions, He will do so truthfully from His faithful heart.[1] But everyone who receives an answer from the Almighty will filter that answer through his or her own value system. We do this all the time. For example, a breakfast cereal claims to lower your cholesterol. You process that claim through your experience and say, "That can't be true. It takes more than a few bowls of cereal to reduce your cholesterol." You may be right, or they may be right. The point is, just as every question is interpreted, every answer is analyzed before it is believed. You will do the same with God's answers to your questions.

FILTERING GOD'S ANSWERS

When your question receives an answer from God, immediately your worldview begins to filter that answer. A worldview is a set of presuppositions and beliefs that you use to interpret and form opinions about everything in your life.

In his book *The Universe Next Door,* James Sire catalogs the most influential worldviews, past and present, that people use to process God's answers to questions. These are Christian Theism, Deism, Naturalism, Nihilism, Existentialism, Eastern Pantheism, and New Age or New Consciousness.[2] Some of these worldviews are still commonly embraced, while others are not currently popular.

Deism, prominent during the eighteenth century, believes in God but postulates that after He created the universe, He abandoned it. This belief is virtually absent from twenty-first-century thinking.

Nihilism is a more recent worldview and believes that there is no value to reality, that life is absurd. To French writer/philosopher Jean-Paul Sartre goes much of the credit (or blame) for this view. Not widely held today, only a few young people and intellectuals admit to being nihilists.

Existentialism is more prominent than nihilism and infiltrates many worldviews, including those of unwitting Christians. While the existentialist also sees life as absurd, nevertheless he or she believes that our choices determine who we are. We create our *own* meaning and value. The world, being meaningless, is what we make of it.

Christian Theism is the worldview presented in the Bible. It holds that God is the Creator and sustainer of all things, that He is a loving God who has a plan to save the world. Because of sin, the world and all those in it need God's salvation.

Naturalism began in the late seventeenth century but gained greater acceptance through Marxism and secular humanism. This worldview believes that God is irrelevant because humanity's progress can be explained by evolutionary change. Thus, man is autonomous and will determine his own destiny. God's answers to our questions are as irrelevant as He is.

New Age Pantheism believes that everything is one and therefore all is God. Human beings are essentially divine, and it is their responsibility to discover the spark of divinity within them. New Age pantheism imbibes traditional pantheistic and Eastern religious practices, including belief in infinite cycles of birth, death, and reincarnation. Had it not been for the Beatles, Shirley MacLaine, and a few other Hollywood people, the Western mind would have rejected this worldview out of hand.

Postmodernism is the worldview of choice in the twenty-first century, although most people don't even know it. More of a mood or condition than a philosophy, postmodernism is much easier described than defined. Postmodernists believe that rules are not valid, authority is not recognized, style is more important than substance, tolerance is the cardinal virtue, words have no inherent meaning, Western culture is always oppressive, and whatever you believe to be right is right.[3] Postmodernism is a reaction to rationalism and absolutism. When you look at postmodern beliefs, you'll recognize that they have permeated our society, even the church.

Obviously, the worldview you use to filter God's answers affects your acceptance of those answers. But, when you ask God a question and He answers, He doesn't answer according to your worldview. God cannot lie. He lays it right out there. You can disregard God's answers, you can debate them, but the one thing you cannot do is deny them. God is on record; His answers to your questions are in print. He couldn't change them if He wanted to.

ACCEPTING GOD'S ANSWERS

Before we get to your questions and God's answers, let's save some "honesty files" to our mental hard drive. Think honestly about the following.

Number one: If you ask an honest person a question, you have to respect that person's answer. You don't have to agree, and you don't have to like it. But if you do ask and the person you ask has a history of being honest, you have to respect that the answer he gives will be an honest one. You don't have to ask again. God has such a history. The Bible shows that God tells the truth. "The LORD is the true God; he is the living God, the eternal King."[4]

You can choose to believe what the Bible says about God or disbelieve it. The one thing you cannot do is deny what the Bible maintains are God's answers to your questions. He will give you an honest answer, even if you don't accept it. Save that file to your mind's hard drive.

Number two: Be honest enough to expect that God's answers will not always parallel your own. You wouldn't expect your friends to answer questions the same way you do. So why would you expect God to answer the same way you do? Do God and you think alike? Not often. In fact, the Bible is quite clear on this point. "'For my thoughts are not your thoughts, neither are your ways my ways,' declares the LORD.

'As the heavens are higher than the earth, so are my ways higher than your ways and my thoughts than your thoughts.'"[5] You should expect that most often His answers will be different than you thought.

Number three: Often when you ask a friend a question, he will pause for a moment, think about your question, and then offer an answer. And when situations change, he revises his answer. But God isn't like that. Recognize that God didn't just think about your question when you asked it. He's known all things for all eternity. In fact, God is on record with His answers. You can read them in His Word, the Bible. That's why in the chapters in which God answers your questions, you will find so many Scripture references at the end of each chapter. God has already responded to your questions, and His answers have been in print for centuries. Save that file to your mind's hard drive.

Number four: Somewhere along the line you'll have to make some judgments. You may read an answer or two from God and say, "I don't believe that" and stop looking for His answers. Barna Research compiled over a thousand questions of your peers, which represent honest questions *to* God that receive honest answers *from* God from the Bible. At some point you'll have to grapple with that.

Are the answers of God likely to supersede the answers of your friends? Who is more apt to know what they're talking about? Part of our problem today is that we live with a "talk radio mentality"—a venue where every opinion is equally valid. But you're a bright person and you know that every opinion isn't equally valid. A pediatric cardiologist is more likely to know how to treat your little brother's heart problem than a gaucho on the Argentine pampas.

You don't have to like God's answers, but they are His answers. They come directly from His Word, the only book God ever wrote. Let God answer for Himself. If you're interested in what He has to say, you've come to the right place. Let down your guard for a while. Set your worldview aside and just let God the Father speak to you in answers compiled from Scripture. Be prepared to be surprised.

Notes

1. Psalm 119:160; Romans 3:4; 2 Timothy 2:13; Titus 1:2; Hebrews 6:13–18.

2. James W. Sire, *The Universe Next Door* (Downers Grove, Ill.: Inter-Varsity, 1988), 18.

3. See Gene Edward Veith, *Postmodern Times: A Christian Guide to Contemporary Thought and Culture* (Wheaton: Crossway, 1994); or Stanley J. Grenz, *A Primer on Postmodernism* (Grand Rapids: Eerdmans, 1996).

4. Jeremiah 10:10.

5. Isaiah 55:8–9; Proverbs 14:12; 16:25.

God's Answers to Your Questions

Predictions

BARNA PROFILE

The most frequently asked questions had to do with what will happen in the days to come. One in ten adults asked something about the future. Those who asked questions about their future were more likely than average to fall into one of the following groups: self-identified Christians, notional Christians, Catholics, those with a high school education or less, or those without particular political affiliations. Although many of their questions were specific and personal, typical questions included:

1) How long will I be healthy?

2) When will I die?

3) When will the world end?

YOUR QUESTION

1) How long will I be healthy?

GOD'S ANSWER

In a perfect world everyone would always be healthy, but you live in a sinful world. People get sick and people die. Some enjoy good health most of their lives and others continuously struggle with health problems. Living in poor health can be a result of making poor choices. Sometimes it has nothing to do with a person's choices.

Sickness and poor health are like I am, in that we show no favoritism.[1] Look at the health history of people whose stories are recorded in the Bible. Children got sick, like the son of the widow of Zarephath, and some died, like King David's son.[2] Kings got sick, like Ben-Hadad, the king of Aram, and Hezekiah, the king of Judah.[3] Prophets got sick, too, like Elisha and Daniel.[4] It is recorded in the New Testament that Epaphroditus and Trophimus were both sidelined from their Christian ministries because of illness.[5] While poor health is not always a person's fault, it is a part of life because the world is still suffering the effects of sin, beginning with Adam and Eve's sin in the Garden of Eden.[6]

What helps a person be healthy? Many people have their own interpretation of what healthy living looks like (as evidenced by the number of books and products available). I will tell you what you ought to do.

Set your body apart as a place of purity. Like the apostle Paul reminded the Corinthian Christians, "Don't you know that you yourselves are God's temple and that God's Spirit lives in you? If anyone destroys God's temple, God will destroy him; for God's temple is sacred, and you are that temple. You are not your own; you were bought at a price. Therefore honor God with your body."[7]

That is a stern warning for anyone who would knowingly do anything to harm his or her body, whether taking drugs, eating gluttonously, or not taking time to rest.[8]

What you put into your body and what you do with it matters. As King Solomon, the wisest man who ever lived, wrote, "If you find honey, eat just enough—too much of it and you will vomit," and, "Like a city whose walls are broken down is a man who lacks self-control."[9] In regard to what you do and what you consume, ask yourself if it is helpful and honoring to Me or if *it* is acting as your master and you its slave.

I have designed a work and rest cycle that can lead to better health. I said to My people of Israel, "There are six days when you may work, but the seventh day is a Sabbath of rest."[10] Setting apart a day to rest is My idea. I rested after creating the world and enjoyed the good that I had made.

Also, many people who stay angry for long periods of time suffer poor health as a result. That's why My Book counsels you to deal with your anger before you go to bed at the end of the day.[11] Prolonged mental anguish is also a certain cause of poor health.[12]

There is a key way to foster a healthy lifestyle that people rarely think of—obeying Me. Through Moses I warned the Israelites when they grumbled at the waters of Marah and Elim: "If you listen carefully to the voice of the LORD your God and do what is right in his eyes, if you pay attention to his commands and keep all his decrees, I will not bring on you any of the diseases I brought on the Egyptians, for I am the LORD, who heals you."[13] While society dismisses the idea, there have been diseases among people that were brought on by lifestyles that were contrary to My laws. Simple obedience is a powerful tool.

YOUR QUESTION

2) When will I die?

GOD'S ANSWER

Many people want to know when they will die, as long as it is not today. Even though you ask, are you sure that you want to know? What would change in your life if you knew? Think on these things.

If you knew you had forty or fifty years left, would you live *today* in a way that matters? Or would you wait a couple of decades before you got serious about living a godly life, figuring you had plenty of time to get ready to die? What if you knew that you only had four or five days to live? What would you do?

King Hezekiah of Judah knew how many years he had until his death. He had been a king who lived to please Me, but he suddenly became ill. The prophet Isaiah went to him and said, "Put your house in order, because you are going to die; you will not recover."[14] That phrase would bring fear to anyone. The king prayed and demonstrated faithful devotion. He wept profusely, and I heard his prayer and let him know he had fifteen more years to live.

If you knew exactly how many years you had left to live,

how would you use that information? After Hezekiah knew, he squandered the remaining years, and they were disastrous. He foolishly showed envoys from Babylon his storehouses and armory, filled with silver, gold, spices, and treasures. His heart was proud, and it became his downfall. Foolish living in the days prior to death is of no benefit to you.

I want you to be prepared to die every day, not just your final day on earth. I want you to ask yourself each morning when you wake up, "What kind of person will I be today? How can I make an effort to better the world I live in?"

One of My servants, Wayne Muller, suggested that there are four great questions all humans face, the third of which is, "How shall I live, knowing that I will die?"[15] Acting on what is significant will make your life worth living.

What are the first priorities in your life and heart?[16] If I were to reveal that you only had a few more days to live, what things would you race to get done? I recommend the following for your "to-do" list:

One: Make sure your relationship with Me is right. That can only happen when you trust what My Son did when He died on Calvary's cross, providing the payment of justice that I require for sins to be forgiven. In light of this first priority, the importance of all others pale in comparison. Read John 3:1–18.

Two: Make sure your relationships with others are right. Is there something between you and your brother or sister, or your mother or father? Have you been living estranged from a friend or family member? Dismiss your pride and go to him or her and talk. Make things right. Get your relationships straightened out before you die. Read Matthew 18:15–19.

Three: Make sure you have made a lasting contribution

with your life. Look around you. What is your legacy? What will people remember you for? Is it the time and energy you put into raising a godly family? Is it the people you helped? What do you want to leave behind? Read Job 29–31.

Four: Make sure you have made an eternal investment. You have only a few moments in this life compared to an eternity to live afterward. Are you now doing what one day you will wish you had done? "Do not store up for yourselves treasures on earth, where moth and rust destroy, and where thieves break in and steal. But store up for yourselves treasures in heaven, where moth and rust do not destroy, and where thieves do not break in and steal. For where your treasure is, there your heart will be also."[17] Read 2 Corinthians 5:6–10.

I haven't told you when you will die because that is not what is best for you. Because I love you, I always do what is best for you. Who else is like Me in this way? But I will tell you that if you aren't prepared to die today, you need to begin to do some serious thinking about "first things." Don't let the "first things" become the last things on your list.

YOUR QUESTION

3) When will the world end?

GOD'S ANSWER

There was a time when the earth did not exist. And there will be another time when it will no longer exist.

"How will the world end?" many ask, receiving all kinds of uninformed answers. According to some scientists' predictions, earth has five billion years, give or take a million, before the sun rapidly expands and engulfs the earth and the other planets. However, most scientists admit that they really don't know how the world will end, nor do they know when.

Who does know? I do. You can read about that day in My Word, in the second letter of the apostle Peter. Here is what he wrote:

The Lord is not slow in keeping his promise, as some understand slowness. He is patient with you, not wanting anyone to perish, but everyone to come to repentance.

But the day of the Lord will come like a thief. The heavens will disappear with a roar; the elements will be destroyed by fire, and the earth and everything in it will be laid bare.

Since everything will be destroyed in this way, what kind of people ought you to be? You ought to live holy and godly lives as you look forward to the day of God and speed its coming. That day will bring about the destruction of the heavens by fire, and the elements will melt in the heat. But in keeping with his promise we are looking forward to a new heaven and a new earth, the home of righteousness.[18]

There are two important statements in these verses that you must not miss. The first is that I do not want anyone to perish. Sin and its consequences did not originate with Me but with Satan, a fallen angel, when his heart was filled with pride and he rebelled against Me. My perfect plan has always been for you to have eternal life.[19] And those who have faith in My Son have My promise that they will not perish but have everlasting life. However, anyone who rejects My Son must face the ultimate consequence of his or her sin, which is death followed by damnation, which is eternal separation from Me.[20]

Second, because of the sin that plagues the world, I will one day destroy it. I will forever separate from Me those who are not "set apart" as Mine. "Set apart" is the definition of the word "holy." Have you accepted My Son and entered My holy kingdom, the family of God? I poured out My wrath upon My Son as He took sinners' place of punishment. Therefore your status is wholly pure and righteous if you accept Him as your Lord and Savior. That is how you can be holy as I am holy.[21] Notice that even though I must destroy the earth in judgment of sin, I will create a new heaven and a new earth, better than the first, untainted by evil.

Some wonder how the world will end. It will end in fire, with an explosion that Peter described as making the "heavens roar." The elements he mentioned refer to matter itself, the "stuff" of the universe. It will melt under the tremendous heat of My fiery judgment. The earth will be laid bare. It will be worse than any imaginable disaster. No living thing or man-made wonder will survive.

So when will this all happen? It starts with the Day of the Lord. If you trace this expression through the pages of the Bible, you will discover that the Day of the Lord is referenced as a time of judgment.[22]

The Day of the Lord refers to the time frame and events that precede the end of the world. Peter said these events would include the physical removal of My followers from the earth, a horrible seven years of tribulation with almost unbelievable suffering and commonplace disasters, and, finally, the messianic reign of Christ when He sits on the throne of David and rules the world from Jerusalem in unprecedented peace for one thousand years.[23] After that thousand years will come the end of the earth and the creation of a new heaven and a new earth. The apostle John, in a vision of that day, said, "Then I saw a new heaven and a new earth, for the first heaven and the first earth had passed away." This account is in Revelation 21.

When will the world end? Look at what has been said. Many things must happen before the earth is destroyed. But *when* the world ends is not nearly as important as My promise to make a new heaven and a new earth—a place you can enjoy with Me forever, if you have a personal relationship with Me that comes through faith in My Son, Jesus Christ. He is the bridge over the separation of sin between you and Me. Will you trust that My Son has paved the way for you to come to Me? That is the issue for you to grapple with. Some are concerned because this world will pass away. Be most concerned that you do not miss your opportunity to trust Christ as your Savior.

Notes

1. Acts 10:34–35; Romans 2:11; Ephesians 6:9.

2. 1 Kings 17:17; 2 Samuel 12:15–19.

3. 2 Kings 8:7; 20:1.

4. 2 Kings 13:14; Daniel 8:27.

5. Philippians 2:26–27; 2 Timothy 4:20.

6. Genesis 3:17–24.

7. 1 Corinthians 3:16–17; 6:19–20.

8. More than 30 percent of American women are obese, more than half don't exercise, and 23 percent of American women still smoke. In

October of 1999, the United States officially passed Japan as the country with the longest annual working hours in the industrial world. In contrast to the citizens of virtually every other industrial nation, Americans are actually working longer hours today than they were thirty years ago. http://www.muextension.missouri.edu/xplor/hesguide/humanrel/gh6656.htm and http://www.organicconsumers.org/Organic/degraaf081202.cfm.

9. Proverbs 25:16, 28.

10. Exodus 20:8–11; Leviticus 23:3. People have failed to rest from the day of old to the present time. It appears to be getting worse as medieval peasants worked less than Americans. As former Labor Secretary Robert Reich pointed out, Americans work nearly one year more during every five-year period than people of other countries. On average, western Europeans enjoy nearly ten years more free time than their American counterparts. http://www.organicconsumers.org/organic/degraaf081202.cfm.

11. Ephesians 4:26–27.

12. A recent study at Kansas State University shows that "Maintaining a negative mood for a long period of time is harmful to your health. People think that getting stressed and anxious is bad for you. The key isn't how stressed you are, but how long you are stressed. Staying stressed for a long time can impair your immune and cardiovascular functions." Scott Hemenover, http://www.eurekalert.org/pub-releases/2002-05/ ksu-goo050902.php.

13. Exodus 15:26.

14. 2 Kings 20:1–18.

15. Wayne Muller, *How, Then, Shall We Live? Four Simple Questions That Reveal the Beauty and Meaning of Our Lives* (New York: Bantam Books, 1997). The other questions are "Who am I?" "What do I love?" and "What is my gift to the family of the Earth?"

16. Author Stephen Covey has become famous for his *First Things First* seminars. Participants take a piece of paper and make a list of the important life roles they have (like friend, parent, boss, or neighbor). Then they write underneath each role names of the people who know them well in that role. Next participants project their life forward, imagining that they are on their deathbed. Covey asks, "What

do you most hope each person would say?" He suggests, "You might, for instance, hope that your children would say something like, 'You loved us fiercely, and we knew it.' Or that your spouse might say, 'I was more whole, joyful, and passionate because you were my life partner.'" Covey challenges the participants to take a good look at what they have written because that is a graphic representation of what really matters to them. These are their "first things," the things they ought to do right now, because they don't know how many more days they have to get them done. See Stephen R. Covey and Rebecca R. Merrill, *First Things First*. audiocassette, February 1996 Covey Leadership Center, 3507 North University Avenue, Suite 100, Provo, Utah 84604.

17. Matthew 6:19–21.

18. 2 Peter 3:9–13.

19. John 3:14–18.

20. Romans 6:23; Revelation 20:10–15.

21. Leviticus 19:2; Matthew 5:48; John 14:19–21; Galatians 2:20.

22. See Isaiah 2:12; 13:6, 9; Ezekiel 13:5; 30:3; Joel 1:15; 2:1, 11, 31; 3:14; Amos 5:18, 20; Obadiah 1:15; Zephaniah 1:7, 14; Zechariah 14:1; Malachi 4:5.

23. The physical removal of Jesus' followers is called the Rapture of the Church. It is depicted in 1 Thessalonians 4:13–18. This is not the Second Coming of Christ because that event takes place at the close of the Tribulation in a breathtaking revelation of Christ's power and glory. The Rapture is a rendezvous before the Tribulation, a rising up of the saved to meet their Lord in the air.

At the end of the seven-year Tribulation, Jesus will come to earth a second time. The first time He came as a baby, born in a Bethlehem stable. The second time will be very different. He will come in power and great glory. The heavens and the earth will shake and human hearts will be seized with fear (Luke 21:25–28; Revelation 19:11–16). He will come to end the terror caused by the Antichrist by engaging him and those who side with him at the Battle of Armageddon; Satan will be tossed into the bottomless pit where he will be confined for the next one thousand years as Jesus reigns on earth (Revelation 19:17–20:7).

Life Purpose

BARNA PROFILE

One in eleven adults (9 percent) asked a question related to their life purpose. Those questioning their life purpose were more likely than average to be: Busters, singles, nonwhites, those who say they have an active faith, born-again Christians, and those in a nonmainline church denomination. These included:

1) Why am I here?

2) What is my purpose in life?

3) What is Your will for my life?

4) Am I living my life the right way?

YOUR QUESTION

1) Why am I here?

GOD'S ANSWER

Throughout history, people have sought answers to the fundamental questions of life such as, "Who are we and why are we here?"

To ask, "Why am I here?" is different than to ask, "What is my purpose in life?" The second is a question of doing. "What must I do to accomplish the purpose for my being?" The first is the ultimate question of being itself. The fundamental question of metaphysics is: "Why is there something instead of nothing?"[1] Searching for answers to the question of being is common to the human race.

So why are you here? Why did I create you? I created you because of who I am, not because of who you are. I, the Father, with the Son and Holy Spirit have existed and will exist as the Trinity of God in three Persons for all eternity. We have perfect, harmonious fellowship. We have never been lonely.

People were not created because I needed them. Some people even presume that I needed someone to boss around. Not true. Domination doesn't bring Me joy. Fellowship with you does. I am a good Father. Joy comes to fathers from loving their children, not dominating them. I have millions upon millions of angels who serve Me.

No, the reason you are here is because of My character. It is innate to My nature to be loving. I am not only the God of love; I am the epitome of love.[2] But this is not just theoretical love. Love is expressed and proved in demonstration. You wouldn't like it if someone said to you, "I love you in theory." As My servant John encouraged Christians, "Let us not love with words or tongue but with actions and in truth."[3] I created you because I am loving. Creation was not so much a demonstration of My power as it was of My love.

I am not, as some have thought, an impersonal force as in "May the force be with you." A force does not desire relationships as I do with My people. I interact with you differently than with the angels, the seraphim, or the cherubim.[4] They are My servants; you are My sons and daughters. The difference in our relationships is like the difference between how a man relates to his heirs and how he relates to his hired hands. He loves both, but he has a special, loving relationship with his children.

I not only created you differently than the angels, but I also created you differently than everything else. You are not a mere assortment of atoms, chemical compounds, and involuntary instincts. Remember where you fit in My creative process. You were not the first of My creation. You were the last. I created light, land, the solar systems, fish, and animals before I created you. You were the crown of My creation, the final chapter.[5] Even the method I used in creating you was distinct. With the rest of creation I simply spoke everything into existence, but with you I used the dust of the earth to form you, and I breathed My divine breath into your nostrils.[6] Adam actually took his first breath from Me. The only other thing that is God-breathed is My Holy Word, the Bible.[7]

So why did I take so much care in creating you? Because you were made in My image, having spiritual qualities. Together We—the Father, Son, and Holy Spirit—fashioned you in Our likeness.[8] More than anyone or anything else, you were created to be like God. All creatures reproduce "according to their kind," and you were created according to the divine kind. You are not divine, mind you, but you were created to relate to the divine.

Why are you here? You are here to have a special relationship with Me. You are not the product of chance or evolution. You are Mine. You are not an accident. You are here because I want you here, and through saving faith in My Son, you can enjoy a loving relationship with Me. As John testified on behalf of those who saw the death and resurrection of My Son, Jesus Christ: "We saw it, we heard it, and now we're telling you so you can experience it along with us, this experience of communion with the Father and his Son, Jesus Christ."[9]

YOUR QUESTION

2) What is my purpose in life?

GOD'S ANSWER

If you live only for what happens in this world, your perspective is going to be quite different from that of someone who plans on living forever in heaven.[10] If you are on your way to heaven, then you have significant, eternal purposes in your life on earth. You'll want others to know the good news of Jesus Christ, saving men from the punishment of their sins. You'll want others to have a relationship with Jesus and be on the way to heaven too.

Machines are only useful if they are used for their intended

purpose. Your computer is a tool to obtain and process information, but it isn't very good food for plants. It wasn't intended to be. In the same way, people are most fulfilled when
they discover the purpose for which I created them. Life has
no purpose without Me, and without purpose you will never
find meaning. Without meaning there will never be significance, and without significance you will never find fulfillment. Your highest fulfillment comes when you are living in a
way that brings glory to Me. That's one reason why I created
you, to reflect My goodness and glory back to Me rather
than for you to be self-indulgent and self-absorbed.

So how do you reflect My goodness and glory back to
Me? One way is through a life of worship. "The LORD is
pleased only with those who worship him and trust his
love."[11] Worship is not a ritual or a recitation; it's an expression of your heart.[12] And worship is not something you only
do in church; it's a lifestyle in which you always seek to reflect My glory back to Me. The apostle Paul said, "So
whether you eat or drink or whatever you do, do it all for the
glory of God."[13] Worship is when you bow your life before
Me and offer everything you are and everything you have to
Me as an act of gratitude. A church reformer, Martin Luther,
said rightly, "A dairymaid can milk cows to the glory of
God." Whatever you do in life, do it in a way that reflects
glory back to Me. That's how you'll find purpose in life.

It was My design for people to be fruitful and increase in
number to magnify My goodness and glory and provide
people with opportunities for fellowship among friends and
family.[14] One of the best ways to enjoy Me is to enjoy the
company of others who enjoy Me. When you trust My Son
as your Savior, you become an adopted member of My large

family.[15] You are My adopted sons and daughters, made holy by My only begotten Son's sacrifice at Calvary. Jesus is unique as My "begotten Son" since He was not made, but He has always been part of the Godhead, both fully God and fully Man.[16] As part of My family, with Myself as your Father and Jesus as your Brother, you will find your life's purpose encouraged through fellowshiping with other members of the family.[17] You help them grow in their faith and they help you. This mutual encouragement is one of your chief purposes in life.[18] It is not good for you to be alone.[19] Enjoy the shared benefits of the family.

But your life has another purpose. I want you to find a niche in service. It was in the heart of My Son to serve Me faithfully while on earth, and your heart will parallel His heart as you willingly serve. The special abilities that you have come from Me, as I am the giver of all good gifts.[20] You can read about these spiritual gifts in several places in the Bible.[21] I have specifically chosen particular gifts for each person so you all will mutually benefit each other in the family. It's important that you know what your gifts are, because whatever I put into you is there to produce a harvest of goodness. Your purpose is to use these gifts to help other members of the family and glorify Me.

You know that with security comes confidence. You can be confident that you are saved from the penalty of your sins and will spend forever with Me if you accept the gift of salvation through Jesus Christ. I want you to spread this good news to others so they become a part of the family too. My Son commissioned you, saying, "Go into all the world and preach the good news to all creation."[22] Your purpose in life is to tell others what is available to them through Jesus

Christ. A person is not only saved from his sins by Jesus' death, but he is given new life as Jesus was given new life when He was resurrected from the dead.[23] The new life available to the Christian is different because My Holy Spirit lives inside him, giving him power and strength to do good works. And the greatest work one can do is help lead another to the truth about new life through Jesus Christ. As My Son told His followers, "All of us must quickly carry out the tasks assigned us by the one who sent me, because there is little time left before the night falls and all work comes to an end."[24]

YOUR QUESTION

3) What is Your will for my life?

GOD'S ANSWER

Many people are confused about My will. Some search for it but do not find it. Others don't care. When people are busy, they easily lose sight of what is eternally important. How you respond to My answer to this question will impact you and others for eternity.

Struggling with My will does not mean that you are spiritually weak. Many of My followers struggle with it. In fact, My Son struggled with My will in the Garden of Gethsemane as He faced crucifixion and the prospect of bearing the sins of the world the next day.[25] But My Son knew His Father's will. Jesus did it because He knew Me and trusted Me.

If you want to know My will, you first have to know Me. The best way to know what someone wants is to know that person really well. People who have known each other for many years don't have much trouble knowing what the other person wants. Although I have always known you inside out (down to the number of hairs on your head), the more intimately you know Me, the more you will know My will.[26] So the best way to begin discerning My will for your life is by getting to know Me better. This will come with time, with fellowship and intimacy. As a husband and wife get to know each other more intimately through time alone together, you need time alone with Me. Put everything else aside for moments alone with Me, and you will discover My will for you.

Another way to get to know Me is by reading the only book I ever wrote, the Bible. The more you read of My Word, the more you discover My will. Did you know that My will is alluded to more than fifty times in the New Testament?[27] The Bible tells you how to test My will and make certain of it.[28] Paul constantly prayed that his friends in Colossae would be filled with the knowledge of My will.[29] John reminded his readers that "The world and its desires pass away, but the man who does the will of God lives forever."[30] Often My Word spells out My will for you:

> *"Therefore do not be foolish, but understand what the Lord's will is. Do not get drunk on wine, which leads to debauchery. Instead, be filled with the Spirit."* (Ephesians 5:17–18)
>
> *"It is God's will that you should be sanctified: that you should avoid sexual immorality; that each of you should learn to control his own body in a way that is holy and honorable, not in passionate lust like the heathen, who do not know God."* (1 Thessalonians 4:3–5)
>
> *"Be joyful always; pray continually; give thanks in all*

circumstances, for this is God's will for you in Christ Jesus." (1 Thessalonians 5:16–18)

"Submit yourselves for the Lord's sake to every authority instituted among men . . . For it is God's will that by doing good you should silence the ignorant talk of foolish men." (1 Peter 2:13, 15)

It was never My intent for My Word to address every situation in life in which you needed to know My will. What has been given in general principles will direct you to discovering My will for each situation.

If you really want to know My will, there is something else you can do. Since those who walk closely with Me absorb My wisdom and understanding, those people can be helpful to you in discerning what I want for your life. King Solomon, one of the wisest people who ever lived, said, "For lack of guidance a nation falls, but many advisers make victory sure," and, "Plans fail for lack of counsel, but with many advisers they succeed."[31] Seeking counsel from several people can help you know My will (and Me) if these people have an intimate relationship with Me. If they don't, you can't always trust their advice.

Many people use their feelings to try and discern My will. They say they have a "hunch" or a "gut feeling." That is foolish. Your feelings are not a good source of guidance. Decisions made while you are sick, tired, depressed, or overworked are more likely to be unwise. Even when you're feeling well, you can't always trust your emotions because they can fool you. King Solomon knew, "There is a way that seems right to a man, but in the end it leads to death."[32] Trusting your feelings can lead to heartache.

I want you to know My will for your life. Sometimes you will struggle to find it and do it, while other times I'll make you wait to receive knowledge of My will. I want *you* to understand that. So what should you do? Get to know Me better while you wait. Spend quality time in My Word to gain understanding of who I am and how I created you to be. Seek counsel from people who are My close companions. And then, when you don't know for sure, act in accordance with My Word and take a step of faith. I'll show you where to go from there.

YOUR QUESTION

4) Am I living my life the right way?

GOD'S ANSWER

Some are unaware or unconcerned that I see every detail of their lives. But what My Word says is true: "Nothing in all creation is hidden from God's sight. Everything is uncovered and laid bare before the eyes of him to whom we must give account."[33] I know exactly how you are living and can show you whether or not it is the right way.

The very word "right" implies some standard of living. For you to know if you are living right means you have to accept some criteria of "rightness." You could do what is right in your own mind and join the chorus of "What's right is what's right for me." But what will you base that on? Your feelings and desires? Those can be sinful and selfish.

What about your conscience? It speaks to you about right and wrong.[34] Your conscience tells you that it is wrong to steal from your employer and take advantage of the elderly. But if you take advantage of the elderly long enough, you become insensitive to that which you know is wrong, and it becomes less unsettling to you. Your perceived benefit outweighs your desire to listen to your conscience. That's what the apostle Paul called having a conscience "seared as with a hot iron."[35] Your conscience can be numbed. Then doing whatever you want can be quite detrimental to yourself and others.

Many people allow society to dictate what is right living. They think that whatever the majority of people are doing must be acceptable or so many wouldn't be doing so. Their moral balances are tipped one way or the other depending on the leanings of their family and friends. Often politicians do this. They vote whichever way the polls indicate is popular with the majority of people, whether that way is right or not. But is the majority able to determine right living? If a poll were taken and the majority of people wanted to call an ant an aardvark, would that make it true? No, and when the majority of people decide to do what is wrong, it is still wrong.

So what is a good guide if you want to know whether you're living right? I have not left you to guess what is right or wrong. I have purposefully moved in the hearts and minds of certain people and inspired them to be writers of My Word, the Bible.[36] I put My thoughts into the minds of these men. The Bible is the guide to living right. "All Scripture is God-breathed and is useful for teaching, rebuking, correcting and training in righteousness."[37] If you want to know whether or not you are living the right way, see if you are following the guidelines I've given you in the Bible.

I have addressed life's challenges in My Book. For example,

in the book of Proverbs, I revealed much truth to King Solomon about right living. This book will help you attain wisdom, get insight and understanding, acquire a disciplined and prudent life, and do what is right, just, and fair.[38] Want to know how to invest your money to receive a high return? Look at the book of Proverbs.[39] Want to know how to choose and keep good friends? Proverbs 18:24 (NKJV) tells you that if you want friends, you have to be a friend to others.[40] Want wisdom to help you choose a spouse and make your marriage last?[41] In fact, there are hardly any challenges you will face in life that I have not addressed in the Bible.

To know if you are living your life the right way, consult My manual daily. That's where you'll discover the truth. Jesus Christ said, "Your word is truth."[42] He also told His followers, "If you hold to my teaching, you are really my disciples. Then you will know the truth, and the truth will set you free."[43] To be freed from a desensitized conscience, to be freed from the hapless opinions of society, to know if you are living your life the right way, get the truth. When you use the right standard, you'll know how to live right.

Notes

1. Philosopher Martin Heidegger, *An Introduction to Metaphysics* (New Haven: Yale University, 1959), 7–8.

2. 1 John 4:8, 16.

3. 1 John 3:18.

4. Psalm 18:6–10; Isaiah 6:1–3; Revelation 5:11–12.

5. Genesis 1:26–31.

6. Genesis 2:7. Martin Luther says that God used a "lump of earth" to fashion Adam.

7. 2 Timothy 3:16.

8. Genesis 1:26; 1 Corinthians 8:6; Colossians 1:15–17.

9. 1 John 1:3 THE MESSAGE.

10. "Cheshire Puss, would you tell me, please, which way I ought to go from here?" asked Alice.

"That depends a good deal on where you want to get to," said the Cat.

"I don't much care where," she answered.

"Then it doesn't matter which way you go," replied the Cat.

—Lewis Carroll, *Alice's Adventures in Wonderland* (New York: Philomel, 1989), 63–64.

11. Psalm 147:11 CEV.

12. Isaiah 29:13.

13. 1 Corinthians 10:31.

"Man's primary purpose is to glorify God and to enjoy Him forever," Douglas Kelly and Philip Rollinson, *The Westminster Shorter Catechism in Modern English* (Phillipsburg, N.J.: Presbyterian & Reformed, 1986), 5. The English Parliament that convened in 1643 drew up a statement of beliefs for the Presbyterian Church of Puritan England. *The Westminster Shorter Catechism* was completed in 1647 by the Westminster Assembly and continues to serve as part of the doctrinal standards of many Presbyterian churches. Scripture proofs used for the first clause of the statement, "Man's primary purpose is to glorify God" are Psalm 86; Isaiah 60:21; Romans 11:36; 1 Corinthians 6:20; and Revelation 4:11. Those texts supporting the second clause, "and to enjoy Him forever" are Psalms 16:5–11; 144:15; Isaiah 12:2; Luke 2:10; Philippians 4:4; and Revelation 21:3–4.

14. Genesis 1:28; 9:1, 7; 28:3; 35:11; 48:4.

15. Ephesians 1:5 NLT.

16. John 3:16, Colossians 1:15–23.

17. Hebrews 2:11.

18. Romans 1:12; Hebrews 10:19–25.

19. Genesis 2:18.

20. James 1:17.

21. Romans 12:5–8; 1 Corinthians 12:4–31; Ephesians 4:7–16.

22. Matthew 28:18–20; Mark 16:15; Luke 24:47–48; Acts 1:8.

23. Romans 6:1–14.

24. John 9:4 NLT. For more on this topic, I recommend Rick Warren's book *The Purpose Driven Life* (Grand Rapids: Zondervan, 2002). He explores five purposes God had in mind in the creation of mankind: 1) Worship—you were planned for God's pleasure; 2) Fellowship—you were formed to be a part of God's family; 3) Discipleship—you were created to become like Christ; 4) Ministry—you were shaped for God's service; and 5) Mission—you were made to tell others about Christ.

25. Matthew 26:36–42; Mark 14:32–36; Luke 22:39–44; John 12:27.

26. Matthew 10:30; Luke 12:7; John 16:13–15; 17:3.

27. Matthew 6:10; 7:21; 12:50; 18:14; 26:42; Mark 3:35; Luke 11:2; 22:42; John 4:34; 5:30 KJV; 6:38, 39, 40; 7:17; 9:31; Acts 13:22 KJV; 21:14; 22:14; 1 Corinthians 1:1; 2 Corinthians 1:1; 8:5; Galatians 1:4; Ephesians 1:1, 5, 9, 11; 5:17; 6:6; Colossians 1:1, 9; 4:12; 1 Thessalonians 4:3; 5:18; 2 Timothy 1:1; Hebrews 10:7, 9, 10, 36; 13:21; 1 Peter 2:15; 3:17; 4:2, 19; 1 John 2:17; 5:14; Revelation 4:11.

28. Romans 12:1–2.

29. Colossians 1:9.

30. 1 John 2:17.

31. Proverbs 11:14; 15:22; 24:6.

32. Proverbs 14:12; 16:25.

33. Hebrews 4:13.

34. Acts 23:1; 24:16; Romans 2:14–15; 9:1; 2 Corinthians 1:12; 1 Timothy 1:5, 19; 2 Timothy 1:3.

35. 1 Timothy 4:2.

36. Exodus 19:7; Leviticus 26:46; Deuteronomy 4:13–14; 2 Kings 17:13; 2 Chronicles 33:18; Psalm 147:19; Ecclesiastes 12:11; Luke 1:68–70; Acts 1:16; 28:25; Romans 3:1–2; 1 Corinthians 2:12–13; 7:10; 14:37; 1 Thessalonians 2:13; 4:1–2; Hebrews 1:1–2; 1 Peter 1:11–12; 2 Peter 1:21; 3:2, 15; 1 John 1:1–5; Revelation 1:1–3, 11, 17–19; 2:7; 22:6–8.

37. 2 Timothy 3:16.

38. Proverbs 1:1–3.

39. Proverbs 3:9–10; 8:18; 10:22; 11:24–25.

40. See also Proverbs 3:27; 12:25; 13:20; 17:9; 19:6; 25:14, 17; 27:5–6, 10.

41. Proverbs 5:19–20; 18:22; 21:9; 30:21–23.

42. John 17:17.

43. John 8:31–32.

Life After Death

BARNA PROFILE

One in twenty adults (5 percent) asked a question about heaven or life after death. The greatest percentage of questioners (74.4 percent) had no active faith. Typical questions included:

1) What happens after I die?

2) What is heaven like?

3) Will I go to heaven?

YOUR QUESTION

1) What happens after I die?

GOD'S ANSWER

What happens after you die depends on your relationship with Me. I did not need permission to create you. "Shall what is formed say to him who formed it, 'Why did you make me like this?' Does not the potter have the right to make out of the same lump of clay some pottery for noble purposes and some for common use?"[1] I created you so I could love you, save you, and give you an eternal home in heaven. I created you so you could enjoy Me and glorify Me. And what happens to you in the future depends on how well you realize what you were created for.

I have plans for you, plans to prosper you and to give you hope and a future.[2] You have the opportunity to embrace My plans or reject them. Your future depends on which course you follow.

One of two scenarios could occur in your future. If you have received by faith My plan to save you, here's what's ahead for you. It is certain that one day you will die unless you live until the day My Son comes to take His followers to heaven with Him.[3] "Man is destined to die once, and after that to face judgment."[4] Death is both universal and certain because it is the consequence of human sin.[5] Death is separation from earthly existence, but the Christian should not fear death.[6] The Christian's soul immediately enters My presence, while the body is placed in the ground.[7] I told Adam that as a result of his sin, "By the sweat of your brow you will eat your food until you return to the ground, since from it you were taken; for dust you are and to dust you will return."[8] That's also true for all of Adam's descendants. But one day I will retrieve your body from the grave and reconstitute it as a body unlike anything you could imagine, a body suited to the atmosphere of heaven where you will live with Me forever.[9] That is what awaits all who have faith in Jesus Christ as their Savior.

Yet what about those who refuse My plan of salvation? If that is you, brace yourself to hear what awaits the rejection of My Son. You, too, will die some day, but what happens immediately after that death is entirely different from what I just described. For you, death seals your fate. I give people plenty of opportunities to respond to the gospel message of salvation through Jesus Christ, but once you have taken your last breath, all chances for salvation have passed. Upon death those who have never accepted Jesus as their Savior will go to a place that the Bible refers to as hades. Hades is not hell, but it might as well be. There is no return from hades; it is where unsaved people go to await bodily resurrection to meet their judgment and final doom.[10]

In the Old Testament, men referred to hades as sheol and sometimes as the "grave" or simply the "pit."[11] Each of those words referred to the same place. However, hades used to have a dimension to it that is not present today. Hades was also the place where saints who died before Jesus' death and resurrection awaited their resurrection. Therefore, there used to be two regions of hades. Now, after My Son's resurrection, the souls of My followers go directly to heaven. But time spent in sheol was different for Old Testament saints and those who rejected Me, who therefore also rejected My Son.

Jesus spoke of two people who died and went to hades.

One was a rich but ungodly man; the other was a poor but godly beggar named Lazarus. The distinction was not their wealth but their relationship with Me. My Son described two halves of hades: one half for the unrighteous and one for the righteous who were waiting to be taken to heaven and who died before Jesus' resurrection. The latter He called Abraham's bosom. (Now the souls of My followers are immediately in My presence; as Jesus said to the man being crucified next to Him, "today you will be with me in paradise."[12]) For the ungodly man in this story, hades was not just a waiting area; he was tormented day and night. Still conscious, he looked up and saw Abraham and the man in the other part of hades. The ungodly man wanted to warn his five brothers so they would not also arrive in hades, so he begged Abraham to send the godly man back to earth to warn these brothers who were destined for the same place of torment. You can read the whole story in Luke 16:19–31.

What happens to you if you die without faith in Christ as Savior? You go to the horrible half of hades and remain there until you are raised from the dead to be judged for your sins. Jesus said, "Do not be amazed at this, for a time is coming when all who are in their graves will hear his voice and come out—those who have done good will rise to live, and those who have done evil will rise to be condemned."[13] All people will one day be raised from the dead, some in the first resurrection, which is the resurrection of the redeemed, and some in the second resurrection, which is the resurrection of the damned. If you have no relationship with Me through faith in My Son, you will be raised in the second resurrection to be judged at the Great White Throne Judgment. There, Christ will perform His role as Judge, as My servant John recorded:

"Then I saw a great white throne and him who was seated on it . . . And I saw the dead, great and small, standing before the throne, and books were opened. Another book was opened, which is the book of life. The dead were judged according to what they had done as recorded in the books."[14]

There are two sets of books here. The second is the Book of Life. This is the record of those who are saved. If your name isn't in that book, it proves that you have rejected My Son and that you belong at this place of judgment. The other set of books (plural) record everything you've ever done in your life. Just as there are degrees of delight in heaven based on acceptable service to Me, there are degrees of punishment based on how wickedly you have lived without Me. "If anyone's name was not found written in the book of life, he was thrown into the lake of fire." This is the second death, and the lake of fire is hell. If you had any idea of how horrible a place it is, you would immediately place your faith in Christ as Savior.

So, back to your question: "What happens after I die?" That depends on you. I set before you two paths. One leads to heaven through Jesus' sacrifice for sins. The other leads away from the cross to hades and eventually to hell. Choose carefully. What happens to you in the future rests on your choice.

YOUR QUESTION

2) What is heaven like?

GOD'S ANSWER

What of My beautiful creation have you seen? There are majestic, snowcapped mountains, rippling streams flowing to flower-studded valleys, and incredible sunsets. All these things are in a world stained by sin. If this kind of beauty remains on earth even though it is tainted with sin, imagine what My home is like![15]

I know how hard it is for you to comprehend My home.[16] A prophet who got just a glimpse of My throne room lamented, "Woe to me! I am ruined! For I am a man of unclean lips, and I live among a people of unclean lips, and my eyes have seen the King, the LORD Almighty."[17] Words are inadequate to describe where I live. The best another prophet could do when describing My home and those around Me was to use similes, saying that it *resembles* this or was *like* that. The apostle Paul said he "heard inexpressible things, things that man is not permitted to tell."[18] Since those who have seen where I live have had trouble depicting it, I will tell you what it is like.

Heaven is My place. It reflects Me, just like your home reflects you. The glory of My presence permeates the whole place. Just as I am holy, separate, and distinct from My creation, everything here, too, is holy, distinct from earth, and without flaw or sin.[19] There is not a single imperfection. My glory is everywhere. I am righteous, and so is everyone here. The souls of men have been made righteous by My Son's death for their sins and His righteousness given to them in the place of that sin. I am the magnificent God, and, as you would expect, everything here is magnificent. Heaven is more than anything you can imagine, resplendent with beauty. Precious stones like jasper, emeralds, sapphires, topaz, and amethyst are everywhere, and the main street of the city is paved with pure gold.[20] There's no place like heaven.

My Son is with Me, seated at My right hand.[21] God the Holy Spirit, God the Son, and I, God the Father, have been here together since before time began. There were thirty-three years when My Son lived among you. But after His death at Calvary's cross, resurrection, and forty days more on earth with His followers, His work on earth was finished, and He came back home. God the Holy Spirit is the Counselor who now lives with and in My followers.[22]

There are many others here with Me, including creatures that enjoy nothing more than praising Me. They say, "Holy, holy, holy is the Lord God Almighty, who was, and is, and is to come," and, "You are worthy, our Lord and God, to receive glory and honor and power, for you created all things, and by your will they were created and have their being."[23] Their greatest fulfillment comes from these genuine acts of worship. There are humans here who began their relationship with Me while on earth but have now died.[24] They praise and thank My Son for what He did. Worship and service bring them great joy. There is an innumerable company of angels here also.[25] And there are many more whom I love still living on earth, who I will one day welcome to My home.

Heaven is *the* most wonderful place. It's filled with much more meaningful activity than you have ever experienced on earth. It's everything good the word *heaven* connotes and more.

YOUR QUESTION

3) Will I go to heaven?

GOD'S ANSWER

This is a very important question. We are talking about your eternal destiny. Do you want to go to heaven when you

die? Heaven is My perfect home, and I don't allow just anyone to come in. Would you allow any stranger who showed
up at your door into your home? I'll tell you what you need
to enter My home.

First, you need to know that trusting in My Son as your
Savior is required. Salvation begins and ends with Me. It is
the result of My love for you. It was demonstrated in a heart-
breaking way at the cross of Calvary. My love shows mercy
instead of administering the deserved punishment, and My
love gives undeserved gifts because I am full of grace.[26]

I love you, not because you are lovable but because I am
love; I don't need to receive but I delight to give.[27] Do you
need somebody to love you today? I'm that Somebody. When
you experience My love, you experience salvation and are on
your way to heaven when you die. But there's more. Once
you have experienced it, you can never be separated from My
love for you.[28] Your destiny is secure.

But there's bad news too. The world needs My love because it is filled with sinners doomed to a horrible eternity
without Me.[29] Evil and sin are all around you. You can think
of many horrid examples. You'd have to be blind or a fool
not to know that you live in a sinful world. Yet you contribute to that sinful world because you, too, are a sinner.
You are a sinner by definition, a sinner by birth, and a sinner
by choice.[30] Hear the decree of My Word about the inclusive-
ness of sin: "For all have sinned and fall short of the glory of
God."[31] Like sheep, you have all gone astray.[32] I, the Lord,
look down from heaven on the sons of men to see if there are
any who understand, any who seek Me. "All have turned
aside; they have together become corrupt; there is no one
who does good, not even one."[33] This is the disease of sin.

Because I am holy (set apart from sin and evil), I cannot permit any unholy or unrighteous person to bring the stain of sin into My home. Because you are a human being who sins, you are both unrighteous and unholy. That's an impasse you can't fix, but I can and I have.

Even though your sin condemns you to death, forgiveness is yours for the taking and accepting.[34] While My holiness demands that I condemn your sin, My love for you has found a way to satisfy My holiness and still make it possible for you to go to heaven when you die. It was a plan conceived in the mind of My Son, My Holy Spirit, and Myself even before We created you or you sinned.[35]

I required a sacrifice to pay the penalty for your sin. That sacrifice had to be innocent and perfect in every way, having no sin, no blemish, and no moral imperfection. Without the shedding of blood, there is no forgiveness of sin.[36] Jesus was your perfect sacrifice whose blood was shed to cover your sin and remove your guilt. He is the only sacrifice that can satisfy My perfect holiness and justice. You could never find such a sacrifice on your own. I provided the sacrifice for you because I love you so much. Jesus Christ is the Lamb of God who takes away the sin of the world.[37] He died in your place and became the only Savior you'd ever need. Read what the Bible says about Jesus' sacrifice for you:

> "For God so loved the world that he gave his one and only Son, that whoever believes in him shall not perish but have eternal life."[38]
> "God (that's Me, God the Father) made him (that's Jesus, God the Son) who had no sin to be sin for us

(humans), so that in him we might become the righ-teousness of God."[39]

"This is how God showed his love among us: He sent his one and only Son into the world that we might live through him. This is love: not that we loved God, but that he loved us and sent his Son as an atoning sacrifice for our sins."[40]

The bad news is, you are a sinner, and I can't allow sinners to stain the perfection of My home. But the good news is that through faith in the sacrifice of My Son at Calvary's cross, you are redeemed, justified, forgiven of all your sins, and on your way to heaven when you die.

So the question remains: "Will I go to heaven?" That's up to you. I've done all that is needed to make it possible. Have you responded to My invitation to come to heaven? Have you stopped trying to even out the bad things you've done with good things? Have you discovered that you cannot make yourself acceptable to Me or earn your way to heaven?[41] Stop trying to do something, and believe that Jesus has provided the way for you to be right with Me.

You can go to heaven when you die and here's how: "Believe in the Lord Jesus, and you will be saved."[42] Have faith that Jesus' death in your place is all that I require of a perfect sacrifice to pay the penalty for your sins. What does it mean to have that kind of faith? It means you believe and accept this good news.[43] When you do, you will be convicted of your sin, feel remorse, and turn away from sin in repentance. That demonstrates that you realize your need for salvation. The key is trusting Me and My plan instead of yourself and your plan.

If you know you must trust Jesus Christ as your own

Savior, and you've never done that before, is there a better time than right now? Don't reject the gift of eternal life by rejecting Jesus and what He did for you. Accept Him and be accepted because His death has paid for your sins. If you reject Him, *that* sin of ultimately rejecting Him will keep you out of My heaven and separated from Me. I want you to choose to be with Me.

Notes

1. Isaiah 29:16; 64:8; Jeremiah 18:6; Romans 9:20–21; 2 Timothy 2:20.

2. Jeremiah 29:11.

3. 1 Corinthians 15:51–58; 1 Thessalonians 4:13–18; Titus 2:11–13.

4. Hebrews 9:27.

5. Romans 5:12; 6:23.

6. Ecclesiastes 9:5, 6, 10; Hebrews 2:14–15.

7. 2 Corinthians 5:8; Philippians 1:20–23.

8. Genesis 3:19.

9. John 14:3; 1 Corinthians 15:35–58.

10. Luke 10:15; 16:19–23; 2 Peter 2:9; Revelation 20:11–15.

11. Genesis 37:35; Numbers 16:30, 33; Job 7:9; Psalm 6:5; Isaiah 14:11.

12. Luke 23:43; 2 Corinthians 5:8; Philippians 1:23.

13. John 5:28–29. The first resurrection includes three separate resurrection events: one, that of the church saints (1 Thessalonians 4:16); two, the precross saints (Luke 13:28; Hebrews 11:13; Daniel 12:2); and three, the Tribulation martyrs (Revelation 20:4; 6:9–11; 7:9–17; 12:17; 13:7, 15; 15:2).

14. John 5:22; Revelation 20:11–15.

15. Genesis 3:17–18.

16. Misguided ideas about heaven:
   Heaven is a place where "for twelve hours every day we will all sing one hymn over and over again."
      —Mark Twain, *Letters from the Earth* (New York: Fawcett, 1974), 17.

"Heaven, as conventionally conceived, is a place so inane, so dull, so useless, so miserable, that nobody has ever ventured to describe a whole day in heaven, though plenty of people have described a day at the seashore."

> –George Bernard Shaw, *Misalliance, The Dark Lady of the Sonnets, and Fanny's First Play: With a Treatise on Parents and Children* (London: Constable, 1914), 39. This quote is from Shaw's *Treatise on Parents and Children.*

17. Isaiah 6:5.

18. 2 Corinthians 12:4.

19. Isaiah 6; Revelation 4–5.

20. Revelation 4:1–6; 21:15–21.

21. Matthew 22:43–44; Mark 14:62; 16:19; Luke 20:42; Acts 7:55–56; Romans 8:34; Ephesians 1:20; Colossians 3:1; Hebrews 1:3; 8:1; 10:12; 12:2; 1 Peter 3:22.

22. John 14:15–21.

23. Revelation 4:8, 11.

24. Revelation 19:1–5; 22:3.

25. Revelation 7:11–12.

26. Isaiah 63:8–9; John 3:16, 15:13; Romans 5:6–8; Ephesians 2:8–10; 1 John 3:16; 4:9–10.

27. "God loves us; not because we are loveable but because He is love, not because He needs to receive but because He delights to give."

> –C. S. Lewis, *Letters of C. S. Lewis,* ed. W. H. Lewis (New York: Harcourt Brace Jovanovich, 1966), 231.

28. John 6:35–40; 10:27–30; Romans 8:38–39.

29. Romans 6:23.

30. Job 14:4; Psalm 51:5. Even the upright Job (Job 1:1) was an imperfect man. He was a saint, but he questioned God's wisdom (Job 3:1–4, 11). He was a pillar of patience, but he became impatient with God and God rebuked him (Job 38–41).

All references in this paragraph are cited in the NKJV. In Hebrew—the language of the Old Testament—sin is called *iniquity* (2 Samuel 22:24 —any action that is not right or straight); *transgression* (Micah 1:5—

a revolt against God); *trespass* (Leviticus 5:15—doing something contrary to one's duty); *unrighteousness* (Leviticus 19:15—any action against God's will; *evil* (Genesis 2:9—anything bad, unpleasant, or disastrous); and *sin* (Deuteronomy 19:15—a clear violation of a command). In Greek—the language of the New Testament—sin is called *disobedience* (Romans 5:19—failing to hear, which results in disobedience); *iniquity* (Matthew 7:23—any act contrary to the law); *transgression* (1 Timothy 2:14—a violation of the law); *trespass* or *offense* (Matthew 6:14—15; Romans 5:15—18, 20—a deviation from what is right or true); *unrighteousness* (Romans 1:18—doing something against God's will); and *sin* (John 1:29—missing the mark, the standard set up by God).

31. Romans 3:23.

32. Isaiah 53:6.

33. Psalm 14:2–3.

34. Romans 6:23; Ezekiel 18:4, 20.

35. Ephesians 1:3–5; 1 Peter 1:18–21.

36. Leviticus 17:11; Hebrews 9:22.

37. John 1:29.

38. John 3:16.

39. 2 Corinthians 5:21.

40. 1 John 4:9–10.

41. Ephesians 2:8–9.

42. Acts 16:31.

43. This is what you need to believe and accept: 1) God loves you even though you haven't returned that love; 2) you have broken God's law, disregarded His Word, and lived as you pleased; 3) there is a severe consequence for your sin—it's your own death; 4) there is nothing you can do to remove the guilt of your sin, but Jesus died to do that for you and to clear the way for you to go to heaven when you die; and 5) you must trust Jesus entirely with your life and your future destiny.

Problems in the World

BARNA PROFILE

One in twenty adults (5 percent) had a question about some type of problem or concern about the world. Those who expressed concern about problems in the world were more likely to be Elders or to reside in the Northeast or Midwest. Typical questions included:

1) Can You help us have peace in the world?

2) Why is there evil?

3) Why is there hatred and crime?

4) Why is there violence and sexual assault?

YOUR QUESTION

1) Can You help us have peace in the world?

GOD'S ANSWER

The issue of war and peace weighs heavily on most hearts today. It does on Mine as well. And the answer to your question, "Can You help us have peace in the world?" is definitely "Yes." That's My plan. If you're puzzled as to why the world is embroiled in so much conflict today, you ought to become better acquainted with My plan in the grand scheme of things.

I revealed My thoughts to over forty individuals over a period of more than fifteen hundred years. Those people were prophets, kings, apostles, and disciples, and I gave them My Word, the Bible. I *inspired* them, which guaranteed that the human writers of the Bible recorded what I revealed to them. There was never an occasion when I promised you world peace. Not one. Certainly there will be periods of less conflict, but there is not a single promise in the Bible that says "lasting" peace will be experienced in your lifetime. Even Jesus, the Prince of Peace, did not promise peace to your world.[1]

The absence of peace in your world is due to the presence of sin. There *was* peace in the Garden of Eden until Satan entered and deceived Adam and Eve. People's desire to brutalize and enslave others comes from within. "What causes fights and quarrels among you? Don't they come from your desires that battle within you? You want something but don't get it. You kill and covet, but you cannot have what you want. You quarrel and fight."[2]

Do you detest war? I do. But in the list of things I hate, war doesn't even make the top ten. In fact, the Bible enumerates twenty-nine things I hate and war isn't listed among them.[3] It's not that I like war, but war is not the greatest of evils. There is something more heinous than war. Injustice. War that ends injustice is better than peace with injustice. I do not view war as the *ultimo ratio*.[4] War is a legitimate response to unchecked injustice. You cannot read the history of My people Israel and think that I oppose all war, for I have at times ordained it.[5]

Yet I can still help you find peace. The Bible calls Me the God of peace, as My Son, Jesus Christ, is the Prince of Peace.[6] I instituted peace in the "peace offering" in Israel's worship ceremony, mentioned eighty-five times in the Old Testament. And the expression "peace from God" occurs fourteen times in the New Testament. So, while I can use war to correct injustice, I am a God who wants you to have peace.

I am the genius behind the greatest peace movement in history. But that movement does not bring the kind of peace most people are expecting; it's something much greater. I have never promised that you will experience world peace, but I have promised you the peace of God. This is personal peace, peace that transcends the understanding of those searching for world peace. I sent My Son to die that you might have peace with Me and that My peace may be in you.[7] He came to guide your feet to the ultimate path of peace.[8] The story of My love for you and My Son's death for you is called the gospel of peace, and rightly so, because it is only through faith in Him you can experience My peace.[9]

Does that mean there will never be world peace? No, there just won't be peace now. One day, Jesus Christ, the

Prince of Peace, will come back to establish an earthly king-dom as Messiah and King.[10] This event is inaugurated by the Second Coming of Christ and the defeat of Satan at the Battle of Armageddon.[11] During My Son's millennium-long rule, there will be no warfare in the world.[12] When Jesus rules in peace, absolute social justice will prevail all over the world, but not until then.

The absence of peace today is due to the presence of sin. Such has been the case from the day Satan introduced sin into your world, and it will continue until the day Jesus Christ comes to crush Satan's rebellion. If you really are in-terested in the world existing in peace, pray the last prayer of the Bible: "Even so, come, Lord Jesus!"[13] When He comes, He will bring peace with Him.

YOUR QUESTION

2) Why is there evil?

GOD'S ANSWER

There are some people today who don't believe that any-thing is evil. They have no standard of right or wrong. Their standard is whatever is evil to them is evil, and whatever is not is not. This is foolish because in the heart of every person there is a conscience that has a sense of right and wrong. Even little children know they shouldn't hit their brother. People are filled with fear when they are speeding and see a police car along the road. That's evidence people know when they are breaking the rules. People can deny the presence of evil, but they're only fooling themselves. They know what evil is.

Evil is described in many ways in the Bible, with a variety of words because there are so many kinds of evil in the world.[14] But let's be clear about one thing. Evil is an absolute thing; it's not just a lesser degree of goodness.[15] I always condemn evil.[16] What's more, it always produces death, both physical and spiritual.[17] I give life; evil takes it away.[18]

So, why is there evil? It didn't come from Me. I created good, not evil. There is one primary source of evil and one secondary source. The primary source is the emperor of evil, Satan himself.[19] It was his pride that initiated evil. Lucifer was one of My angels, but he thirsted for more. The words recorded by Isaiah describe Lucifer's self-destruction. He was the morning star, the son of the dawn. He once served Me faithfully, but then he wanted to not only be like Me but also be above Me. With a proud heart he vowed, "I will ascend to heaven; I will raise my throne above the stars of God; I will sit enthroned on the mount of assembly, on the utmost heights of the sacred mountain. I will ascend above the tops of the clouds; I will make myself like the Most High."[20] It didn't happen. Instead Lucifer destroyed himself and brought evil into the world. He was allowed to choose evil and disobey Me as you are also given that choice.

The pride in Satan's heart that drove him to lead a rebellion against Me is the primary source of evil in the world. But there is a secondary source. It is the human heart. When Adam sinned in the Garden of Eden, he joined in on Satan's rebellion. As the representative head of the human race, his sin was your sin. It is like sending a representative from your district to Congress. That representative acts and speaks for you. Your congressman casts a vote for you. Don't be critical of Adam for falling into sin. He did exactly what you would have done had you been there. Adam was the original sinner, but every person descended from Adam is also sinful.[21] Every sinful parent (and that's every parent) gives birth to an innately sinful child.[22] So you are sinful both by birth and by choice.

Yet, the following good news must not be missed: Even though by the sin of one man, Adam, death reigned through that one man to all men, the gift of righteousness reigns in life through the one man, Jesus Christ. Just as the result of one sin was condemnation for all men, so also the result of one act of righteousness (Christ's death on the cross) was justification that brings life for all men. For just as through the disobedience of the one man, the many were made sinners, so also through the obedience of the one man (Christ), the many will be made righteous.[23]

Though you have the good news, I have more to say about evil. You know *why* there is evil, but do you know how sinful the human heart is? The prophet Jeremiah asked, "The heart is deceitful above all things and beyond cure. Who can understand it?"[24] Who can understand the heart of horrible men who have murdered thousands? Can you even understand your own heart? It is evil as a murderer's heart is evil. "This is the evil in everything that happens under the sun: The same destiny overtakes all. The hearts of men, moreover, are full of evil and there is madness in their hearts while they live, and afterward they join the dead."[25] Every human heart is evil and deserving of condemnation, even though every heart does not equally act on that evil. Anyone who breaks one of My laws is guilty of breaking them all.[26]

Until I make a new heaven and a new earth, evil will continue. You can read about this new eternal state in the last two chapters of the last book of the Bible. Yet evil within the hearts of men persists because your understanding has been darkened by sin.[27] But even though your heart is innately evil, I can give you a new heart. I'm not talking about a physical heart transplant. I'm talking about a new heart spiritually. To My stubborn people Israel I promised, "I will give you a new heart and put a new spirit in you."[28] How can I do that? My Holy Spirit softens your heart and opens it to respond to the message of the gospel.[29] And then it happens. You recognize the truth of My Word, you believe it in your heart, confess it with your mouth, your sins are forgiven, and you are saved from the penalty of your sin.

Here's how Paul described this change of heart in Romans 10:9–10: "That if you confess with your mouth, 'Jesus is Lord,' and believe in your heart that God raised him from the dead, you will be saved. For it is with your heart that you believe and are justified, and it is with your mouth that you confess and are saved." It's not just a change of heart; it's a change of destiny as well. It's going from a hard heart to a holy heart, and from hell to heaven, just by believing the gospel message of good news.

I remove the guilt of your sins, so don't let Satan accost you with false guilt for sins that you have turned away from that I have forgiven.[30] Guilt brings you to repentance, but after the sin is confessed it has served its purpose.[31]

Why is there evil? Because of Satan and the sinfulness of the human heart. What can destroy evil inside your heart? Believing in Jesus as Savior and confessing Him as Lord. That's the miracle of salvation, and it can happen to anyone who believes. Evil is here to stay for now, but with a new heart, it won't rule your life.

YOUR QUESTION

3) Why is there hatred and crime?

GOD'S ANSWER

By reading My answers to your other questions like "Why is there evil?" you'll see a consistency in My responses. Most of the evils in your world have the same origin. I created a wonderful world, free from evil, fear, hatred, and crime. Everything was beautiful and peaceful. But when Satan came to Eve, tempted her, and she and Adam fell into Satan's trap of sin, bad things began to happen. Soon there was hatred. There was disease. There was crime. There was illness. There was death. None of these existed in the world before that. Crime is one of those results of sin entering the world.

Anyone who can see knows that hatred and crime are problems in the world. Thoughts of certain names and places conjure up images of horror. Saddam Hussein used chemical weapons on both his neighbor Iran and on his own people, the Kurds, killing thousands.[32] War crimes are also caused by hatred.

America has not escaped the sin of hatred either. The number of hate crimes in your nation is increasing.[33] Most of the hatred takes place between different racial and religious groups.

I created you with emotions and gave you the ability to hate as well as love. There are many things that the Bible mentions that I hate. In fact, Proverbs 6:16–19 lists seven of them: "haughty eyes, a lying tongue, hands that shed innocent blood, a heart that devises wicked schemes, feet that are quick to rush into evil, a false witness who pours out lies and a man who stirs up dissension among brothers." These are all worthy of hatred. So if I hate something, shouldn't you hate it too? "Let those who love the LORD hate evil."[34]

"To fear the LORD is to hate evil; I hate pride and arrogance, evil behavior and perverse speech."[35] There is a litany of things in My Word that those who claim to love Me should hate.[36] So hatred itself is not wrong, but hating the wrong thing is. Racial hatred is not right. Ethnic or cultural hatred is not right. Religious hatred is not right. The reason so many people are confused about hatred is that many of them hate what I love and love what I hate.

There are sinners who do not mind taking what is not theirs or killing to have their own way. All of this can be traced to one source—the entrance of sin into your world. Because of the Fall of man, when Adam and Eve first sinned and a sinful nature became something each subsequent person inherited, there have been sinful things in the world that *ought* to be hated. However, hating what you *ought not* to hate is also a sin that continues to plague people.

Often people who love what I hate accuse those who hate what I hate of committing hate crimes. They are not making a right judgment. To speak out against what I hate is not a hate crime; My prophets did that all the time. But hating what I hate and committing crimes against those who do what I hate are not the same. I hate sexual immorality in every form—sodomy, adultery, homosexuality, fornication, and bestiality. Even though I hate these things, it is sinful for people to do other things that I hate in response. My Son made that very clear when He said, "You have heard that it was said, 'Love your neighbor and hate your enemy.' But I tell you: Love your enemies and pray for those who persecute you."[37] And He was not the first to suggest that you do not reciprocate hatred. Moses said, "If you see the donkey of someone who hates you fallen down under its load, do not leave it there; be sure you help him with it."[38]

Solomon agreed, saying, "Hatred stirs up dissension, but love covers over all wrongs."[39] You can hate what I hate and still demonstrate My love to your enemies.

Have you not heard it said, "Love the sinner and hate the sin"? What's more, if you love Me, you are to love others as well, even those who hate you. If you do not love those who hate you, you can never legitimately claim to love Me. "Anyone who claims to be in the light but hates his brother is still in the darkness."[40]

"If anyone says, 'I love God,' yet hates his brother, he is a liar. For anyone who does not love his brother, whom he has seen, cannot love God, whom he has not seen."[41] You show that you love Me by loving those who hate you.

Just because you love Me and others, don't expect others to love you in return. It's not going to happen. Jesus said, "If the world hates you, keep in mind that it hated me first. If you belonged to the world, it would love you as its own. As it is, you do not belong to the world, but I have chosen you out of the world. That is why the world hates you."[42] And John the apostle concurred: "Do not be surprised, my brothers, if the world hates you."[43]

So if you're looking for the real perpetrators of hate crimes today, look at those who persecute My people and hate what is good. Hatred is a horrible thing in the hearts of those who do not have the Spirit of God, for they do not know what to love and what to hate.

Why is there crime? Because each human being is a criminal at heart. My prophet Jeremiah said, "The heart is deceitful above all things and beyond cure. Who can understand it?"[44] Often those who commit violent and nonviolent crimes don't even know why they do it. But I do. People commit crimes because of their natural bent toward sin. You don't have to teach a child how to steal, but you do have to teach him how to be honest. Sin permeates all human beings— body, soul, and spirit—and what you find inside of a person is what will come out in times of desperation or opportunity. When you cut your finger, you bleed. What comes out is blood because that's what's on the inside. When the opportunity to commit a crime is presented to sinful humans, they struggle to keep what's inside from coming out.

There is much written about crime and punishment in My Word. Even though the penchant to sin is a part of your makeup, I have commanded those who love Me to live with that penchant in check. "Be holy because I, the LORD your God, am holy."[45] Remember the Ten Commandments: You shall not murder; you shall not steal; you shall not covet what belongs to your neighbor . . .[46] I expect people to treat others with respect and fairness and not to cheat them or steal from them.[47] I also expect people to respect life and not purposefully take the life of another.

However, your society must not fail in exercising its responsibility to administer punishment to crime. Such punishment should demand justice and yet at the same time demonstrate compassion toward the offender. Even before there were governments and justice systems, I ordained punishment for those who committed crime. That punishment, however, was within well-defined bounds.[48] My law says that punishment should both fit the crime and be no less severe than the crime.[49] But it also says that justice is not served if the punishment is more severe than the crime or fails to take into account the motives and intent of the criminal.[50]

Crime without punishment is not justice. But justice without compassion is not genuine justice either. My Son had compassion toward prisoners.[51] I am attuned to the cries of those in prison when they call out to Me with a sincere heart.[52]

Some day, crime and punishment will be a thing of the past. My Son's messianic rule on earth will be what people are looking for today but cannot find because there is still sin in their hearts.[53] Until the day Jesus rules with fairness, faithfulness, and justice, there will be crime.[54] However, with Satan and his demon agents bound, people's penchant for crime will be held back forever. And one day, in heaven, those penchants will be gone forever. Then crime will be gone forever, and punishment will be history. And crime-free, fear-free peace will finally be here.

YOUR QUESTION

4) Why is there violence and sexual assault?

GOD'S ANSWER

Why is there violence? I have a guide for people to get along, but it is often ignored. Some people act more like wild animals than people created in My image. That's why there's violence. Compare Genesis 1–3 with Genesis 4–6. In the beginning, there was no violence. Everything was orderly. I purposely created your universe in an orderly fashion. Light appeared first, before plants, because green plants need photosynthesis to live. The animals, created after the plants, needed the oxygen from those plants to breathe. My creation was not only skillful and amazing, but also it was sequential and intelligent.

But everything changed. Sin entered your universe and with it came pain, suffering, and violence. Cain became angry because his offering was not looked upon with favor. He attacked his brother, who had given a favorable offering, and murdered him. Next he lied to Me about it. Cain became a restless, wandering exile.[55] The contrast between the tranquility of Genesis 1–3 and the turmoil of Genesis 4–6 is striking. It also reflects why there is violence in your world today.

Violence in America is an epidemic. So much of the violence in your land is both youth oriented and sex oriented. Every two minutes in America, someone is sexually assaulted.[56] Of course, youth-related violence is not new. The Bible records frequent incidents of violence among younger people. Absalom was a young man when he arranged to have his half brother Amnon murdered.[57] Teen violence has since exploded into disastrous proportions.[58]

Much violence is sex related. Acquaintance and date rape have become scourges of university campuses.[59] I detest all sexual crimes, such as child abuse, abduction, and torture.

I created humanity as male and female.[60] My plan from the very beginning was that males and females would be different so they would complement each other. I created sex so males and females would experience the pleasure of physical intimacy and would perpetuate their race. And look what has happened. Sin has so corrupted men and women that today what I designed to be enjoyed through marriage for a lifetime relationship has become cheapened and sometimes even violent.[61] I gave people love, and they settled for lust.

Do you think that people can watch violence without becoming desensitized or a perpetrator of it? Why would a person believe he could watch indiscriminate sex on television or in movies and not be tempted by or become more numb to indiscriminate sex?[62] The Internet has provided further opportunities for people to view sexual violence.[63] Much of what was considered pornographic two decades ago is now seen as acceptable media. Even the most liberal sociologists who do not know Me have abandoned foolish notions that there is no link between pornography and violent sexual behavior.[64]

Can anything be done to stop the violence, especially sexual violence? Yes, but don't expect your government or educational institutions to do it. Sexual violence is out of control. Don't expect the media to care. When they exploit violence and sexuality, their ratings skyrocket. So what can a parent do to curb sex-related violence? For one, parents can rightly capitalize on their responsibility to tell their own children about sex. How will kids have a godly, healthy attitude toward sex if it is not proactively instilled? Do you know where most children today learn about sex? Television.[65]

There are many twisted views about the purpose of sex. Parents, you can teach your children the truth. I have given you the responsibility of raising your children so they are fed My Word. If you abdicate that responsibility, don't curse the darkness. Your children had an inadequate foundation. Don't begin too late to mold them into nonviolent people who have appropriate respect for others and their bodies.

Talk to your children, especially your sons, about their attitudes toward members of the opposite sex. Much of the violence against women today is fostered by the degenerating attitudes of society. Falling levels of morality have produced more unhealthy male attitudes toward women. As long as people use sex to sell their products and the media portrays violence as exciting and normative, you will face an uphill battle in curbing violence in your community. But you can nurture your sons' hearts to love God and respect women. "What comes out of a man is what makes him 'unclean.' For from within, out of men's hearts, come evil thoughts, sexual immorality, theft, murder, adultery, greed, malice, deceit, lewdness, envy, slander, arrogance and folly. All these evils come from inside and make a man 'unclean.' "[66] Don't let the media desensitize your sons toward women and sex. Don't let young girls be trained to become women who try to fill the deepest longings of their souls with idols of relationships, romance, and sex. Have heart-to-heart talks with them so you can help them guard their minds and hearts.

One day the violence, shootings, and sexual brutality will stop. But that day hasn't come yet. It won't come until My Son rules on the earth, until "the kingdom of the world has become the kingdom of our Lord and of his Christ, and he will reign for ever and ever."[67] Until the coming of Christ's millennial kingdom on earth and eternal kingdom to follow, teach your children respect and help them live in My peace. That will make your home an attractive place where your children will want to find solace from the violent world around them.

Notes

1. Isaiah 9:6; Matthew 10:34–40.

2. James 4:1–2.

3. God hates: detestable pagan practices (Deuteronomy 12:29–31); pagan Asherah poles (Deuteronomy 16:21); pagan sacred stones (Deuteronomy 16:22); all who do wrong (Psalm 5:5); the wicked and those who love violence (Psalm 11:5); haughty eyes, a lying tongue, and hands that shed innocent blood (Proverbs 6:17); a heart that devises wicked schemes and feet that are quick to rush into evil (Proverbs 6:18); a false witness who pours out lies and a person who stirs up dissension (Proverbs 6:19); heartless New Moon festivals and feasts (Isaiah 1:14); robbery and iniquity (Isaiah 61:8); burning incense to pagan gods and worshiping other gods (Jeremiah 44:3–4); Israel's wickedness in Gilgal (Hosea 9:15); sin-tainted religious feasts and sin-tainted assemblies (Amos 5:21); the fortresses of corrupt, prideful Israel (Amos 6:8); plotting evil against your neighbor and swearing falsely (Zechariah 8:17); Edom, the descendants of Esau (Malachi 1:2–3; Romans 9:13); divorce and unfaithfulness to a wife (Malachi 2:16); the practices of the Nicolaitans (Revelation 2:6, 15).

4. *Ultimo ratio* means last recourse. The motto that the Prussian leader Frederick the Great (1712–86) had inscribed around the mouths of his cannons was the *Ultimo ratio.* The full motto is *ultimo ratio regum—* the last recourse of kings. Swiss theologian Karl Barth, in his multi-volume *Church Dogmatics,* insisted that war was the *ultimo ratio,* something that is subhuman and never noble or virtuous.

5. While Israel entered many unadvised wars without the blessing of God, there are many examples of wars that God sent Israel to fight. For example, God ordained war against the tribe of Benjamin (Judges 20), war with Amalek (1 Samuel 15:1–9), and war with the Philistines (2 Samuel 5:17–25; 1 Chronicles 14:8–17).

6. Isaiah 9:6; Romans 15:33; 16:20; 1 Corinthians 14:33; Philippians 4:9; 1 Thessalonians 5:23; Hebrews 13:20–21.

7. Romans 5:1; Colossians 3:15; John 14:23–27.

8. Luke 1:67–79.

9. Romans 10:15 NKJV; Ephesians 6:15.

10. Isaiah 4:2–6; Revelation 20:1–6.

11. Matthew 24:29–30; Revelation 19:11–21.

12. Psalm 46; 72; Isaiah 2:4; 11:6–16; Micah 4:1–8.

13. Revelation 22:20 NKJV.

14. There are at least six different Hebrew words used for "evil" in the Old Testament. The various words mean failure (Deuteronomy 19:15), crooked (2 Samuel 22:24), rebellion (Micah 1:5), faithlessness (Leviticus 5:15), unrighteousness (Leviticus 19:15), and evil (Genesis 2:9). Similarly, at least six different Greek words are used for evil in the New Testament. The various words mean missing the mark (John 1:29), failure to hear (Romans 5:19), lawlessness (Matthew 7:23), deviation (Matthew 6:14–15), deception (1 Timothy 2:14), and unrighteousness (Romans 1:18).

15. Genesis 2:9; 1 John 1:5–10.

16. Matthew 11:20–24; 23:13–14; Mark 3:28–29. The latter verse brings up blasphemy against the Holy Spirit. This blasphemy (to misuse, reject, or despise the truth of God) is unforgivable because it is the Holy Spirit who brings us truth of the good news of Jesus' death and resurrection, which saves us from our sins. If we reject Jesus, our only hope of salvation from our sins, we have committed blasphemy against the Holy Spirit who testifies to this truth. That eternal sin is unforgivable.

17. Genesis 2:17; Galatians 6:7–8; James 1:13–15.

18. John 5:21–26; Ezekiel 18:20.

19. Satan's pride was his downfall as indicated in 1 Timothy 3:6. Likening a ruler of ancient Tyre to Satan, the prophet Ezekiel describes how Satan came to generate evil. See Ezekiel 28:1–19.

20. Isaiah 14:12–17. Some angels decided to follow Satan in his rebellion. Revelation 12:3–4 may be an indication that one-third of the angels fell with Satan. The war in heaven between God's angels and Satan's angels is described in Revelation 12:7–12.

21. Romans 5:12.

22. Job 14:1–4; Psalm 51:5.

23. Romans 5:17–19.

24. Jeremiah 17:9.

25. Ecclesiastes 9:3.

26. James 2:10.

27. Ephesians 4:18.

28. Ezekiel 36:26.

29. John 6:44, 65; 10:1–16; Acts 16:14; 1 Thessalonians 5:23–24.

30. John 8:44; Revelation 12:9–10.

31. 2 Corinthians 7:10–11; Hebrews 10:1–2; 22.

32. The Iran-Iraq war produced 1.5 million casualties during eight years of hostilities. The war was the first time since the interwar years that chemical weapons were used in combat. Beginning in 1984, and almost certainly by 1986, Saddam Hussein used chemical weapons on the battlefield against Iranian troops. When the war wound down, Saddam began a campaign against a Kurdish insurgency in the north. In that campaign he again turned to chemical weapons, using a combination of mustard gas and nerve gas that killed some 5,000 civilians in the town of Halabja in August 1988. As in his war with Iran, Saddam's use of chemical weapons (this time against civilian targets) failed to raise outrage in the world community. Toward the end of the war, the Iraqi regime pursued its genocidal *Anfal* policy, killing between 50,000 and 200,000 and destroying about 3000 Kurdish villages.

33. The FBI's annual publication *"Crime in the United States 2001"* reports that while the overall number of crimes reported to the FBI in 2001 increased slightly (2.1%), reported hate crimes increased dramatically from 8,063 in 2000 to 9,726 in 2001 (a 20.6% increase). In 2001, 1,663 more hate crime incidents were reported than in 2000. Racial bias again represented the largest percentage of bias-motivated incidents (44.9%), followed by ethnic/national origin bias (21.6%), religious bias (18.8%), sexual orientation bias (14.3%), and disability bias (0.3%).

34. Psalm 97:10.

35. Proverbs 8:13.

36. The Bible tells us that we are to hate every wrong path (Psalm 119:104, 128), those with divided loyalties (Psalm 119:113), those who hate the LORD and those who rise up against Him (Psalm 139:21–22). The righteous hate what is false (Proverbs 13:5), hate evil, and love good (Amos 5:15).

37. Matthew 5:43–44.

38. Exodus 23:5.

39. Proverbs 10:12.

40. 1 John 2:9.

41. 1 John 4:20.

42. John 15:18–19.

43. 1 John 3:13.

44. Jeremiah 17:9.

45. Leviticus 19:2; 1 Peter 1:16.

46. Exodus 20:1–17; Deuteronomy 5:6–21.

47. Leviticus 19:32–36; Proverbs 11:1; 16:11; 20:23.

48. Genesis 4:11–16.

49. Genesis 9:6; Leviticus 24:17; Numbers 35:16–18.

50. Numbers 35:9–12, 22–25.

51. Matthew 25:36; Luke 4:18–19.

52. Psalm 68:6; 79:11; 102:19–20.

53. Psalm 72:8–11; Revelation 20:1–6.

54. FBI crime figures show that violent crimes in America increased only marginally in 2000, but as professor James Alan Fox of Northeastern University in Boston said, "I cannot imagine any clearer indication that the crime drop is over." Source: http://www.usatoday.com/news/washington/2001-05-30-crime-stats.htm. Motor vehicle theft rose 2.7 percent and larceny-theft increased 0.1 percent. In some categories, the reversals were profound. For instance, murders in big cities with more than one million residents rose 2.5 percent in 2000.

55. Genesis 4:1–16.

56. RAINN calculation based on 2000 National Crime Victimization Survey. Bureau of Justice Statistics, U.S. Department of Justice.

57. 2 Samuel 13:28–29.

58. The Centers for Disease Control reports that more than four hundred thousand youth ages ten to nineteen were injured as a result of violence in the year 2000 (CDC 2001a). In 1999, 82 percent of homicide victims 15 to 19 years old were killed with firearms (CDC 2001a). Source: CDC. Youth Risk Behavior Surveillance—United States, 2001. *MMWR* 2002; 51 (SS-04) 1–64.

59. One in four college women has been raped; that is, has been forced, physically or verbally, actively or implicitly, to engage in sexual activity. A 1985 study revealed that 90 percent of college rape survivors knew their attacker before the incident. Source: http://ubcounseling. buffalo.edu/violenceoverview.shtml#facts.

60. Genesis 1:27; 5:2.

61. Genesis 2:18–24; Mark 10:6–9.

62. Even those programs that are not explicitly sexual have so much embedded sexual content that the producers aren't fooling anybody, except perhaps the U.S. Supreme Court. "Embedded sexual content" is sexual content embedded within a larger context that includes considerable nonsexual content. Soap operas include a story line that is not exclusively sexual but often portray sexual interactions in the script. *Playboy* magazine includes considerable nonsexual content (e.g., interviews with jazz artists) but also includes nude photographs http://www.dianarussell.com/porncirculation.html.

63. Barron and Kimmel recently measured the levels of sexually violent content in representative samples of sexual magazines, videos, and Internet sex-story sites. They found that the Internet content was significantly higher in violence than were videos or magazines. The other media contained only 2 percent of "extreme" forms of violence, but the Internet contained 17 percent. M. Barron and M. Kimmel, "Sexual violence in three pornographic media: Toward a sociological explanation," *Journal of Sex Research* 37 (2000): 166.

64. It is estimated that 25–30 percent of male students admit that there is some likelihood they would rape a woman if they could be assured they would get away with it. However, 57 percent said they would likely perform a violent rape after exposure to sexually violent images. Edward Donnerstein, unpublished transcript of testimony to the Public Hearings on Ordinances to Add Pornography as Discrimination

against Women (Committee on Government Operations, City Council, Minneapolis, MN, 1983, pp. 4–12). Donnerstein noted that the relationship between pornography and violence against women is stronger than the relationship between smoking and lung cancer.

65. According to a 1998 *Time*/CNN poll, 29 percent of U.S. teens cited television as their principle source of information about sex, up from 11 percent in a similar poll conducted in 1986. While 45 percent mentioned "friends" as their major source, only 7 percent of teens identified their parents as having told them about sex. Neil M. Malamuth and Emily A. Impett, "Research on Sex in the Media: What do we know about effects on children and adolescents?" in D. G. Singer and J. L. Singer, eds., *Handbook of Children and the Media* (Thousand Oaks, Calif.: Sage, 2001), 270–71.

66. Mark 7:20–23.

67. Revelation 11:15.

Suffering

BARNA PROFILE

Questions related to suffering were mainly about why it exists or why God allows it. These questions were asked by 5 percent of adults. Those concerned about suffering were most likely to be female. Typical questions included:

1) **Why do bad things happen to me?**

2) **Why did You take my loved one from me?**

3) **Why do You allow hunger?**

YOUR QUESTION

1) Why do bad things happen to me?

GOD'S ANSWER

Bad things happen to you because you live in a sinful world. From the very moment Adam and Eve disobeyed Me in the Garden of Eden, they brought sin and death into the world. They exchanged beauty for ashes. Notice the record in the first chapter of the Bible that describes how I gave My appraisal of what I created. When I finished it all, I saw that it was all *very* good.[1] You are not blaming the right person if you blame Me for your troubles.

It wasn't long after Adam and Eve sinned that bad things began to happen in your world. One of their sons, Cain, killed another of their sons, Abel.[2] Murder was one of the world's earliest crimes. Other things adversely impacting your world like lying, polygamy, war, sodomy, famine, and hypocrisy followed.[3]

No one is exempt from the effects of sin, not even a godly person. One of My closest followers, a dedicated Christian, an apostle in the first century—his life was riddled with bad things happening to him. Paul suffered horribly at the hands of the Romans and the Jews. For his faith he was imprisoned, flogged, shipwrecked, and denied basic needs like food, shelter, sleep, and clothing.[4] Even though he described himself as being "in weaknesses, in insults, in hardships, in persecutions," he said he took great delight in these things because they happened for the sake of his Lord and Savior, Jesus Christ.[5] When Paul was weak, Christ was strong through him. Paul didn't enjoy pain. Rather, he delighted in the privilege of serving Me regardless of the bad things that happened to him.

I am close to the brokenhearted and save those who are crushed in spirit.[6] No one cares for you more than I do because no one loves you more than I do. Jesus asked a rhetorical question to assure His followers of His care and concern. He said, "Are not two sparrows sold for a penny? Yet not one of them will fall to the ground apart from the will of your Father. And even the very hairs of your head are all numbered. So don't be afraid; you are worth more than many sparrows."[7]

My Son warned you to expect pain and trouble in your life, but He also encouraged you, "I have told you these things, so that in me you may have peace. In this world you will have trouble. But take heart! I have overcome the world."[8] When Jesus returns and establishes Himself as King, He will rule over the earth in a way that reflects My benevolent and wise authority.[9] He will lift the divine curse on creation and cleanse the earth of its pollution, restoring it to beauty and fertility.[10]

Hope is available to you, even in the midst of bad times, because I have not abandoned you. Paul, who was killed by the sword of Nero, the emperor of Rome, encouraged you, saying, "My friends, we want you to understand how it will be for those followers who have already died. Then you won't grieve over them and be like people who don't have any hope. We believe that Jesus died and was raised to life. We also believe that when God brings Jesus back again, he will bring with him all who had faith in Jesus before they died."[11]

Adopt Paul's eternal perspective: "I consider that our present sufferings are not worth comparing with the glory that will be revealed in us."[12] But the real question is not of limitation; it's the question of allowance. Why do I allow you to go through hard times? It is the same reason I allow darkness to fall each night and clouds to form on some sunny days. I have plans for that darkness and for those clouds. And My plans are bigger than giving you a momentary sunset or a silver lining of clouds. I'm the kind of God who doesn't keep you from hard times if those hard times will ultimately benefit you.

The story of Joseph in the Old Testament is one of the greatest stories of tragedy turned triumph. The goodness of the triumph far outweighed the distress of the tragedy. Joseph never lost faith that I was with him and would turn his hard times to his ultimate good. He never gave up. After all his hard times were over, he said to his brothers, "You intended to harm me, but God intended it for good to accomplish what is now being done, the saving of many lives."[13] That is My intention—your good and the good of others. I would not allow you to go through hard times for no reason.

Romans 8:28 is a promise to all whom I love who are going through tough times. It says: "In all things God works for the good of those who love him, who have been called according to his purpose."

YOUR QUESTION

2) Why did You take my loved one away from me?

GOD'S ANSWER

You've lost someone very dear to you. I know how you feel. I vividly remember the day I watched My Son suffer at the hands of arrogant religious leaders and die at the hands of Roman soldiers. Worst of all, as He was dying on the cross, I had to turn My face away from Him.[14] He was bearing the sins of the world and He had to do it alone.[15] I know the pain you feel.

Think about death and why it happens. As soon as human beings draw their first breath, each subsequent breath brings them closer to death than their last. It wasn't the death of your loved one that surprised you and caused you to grieve. It was its timing. All people die; you just don't know when. I didn't *take away* the person you loved; death took him or her. That's an important distinction. I am the giver of life, not the taker of life. Human death is the consequence of sin.[16] Sin, beginning with Adam's sin, brought death to everyone, including your loved one.[17] But My offer of eternal life and hope is available to everyone.[18]

I will not offer you any of the false consolations that people often give to those who lose a loved one. I will not offer you the pious explanations that My servant Job's comrades offered him. They didn't satisfy Job, and they won't satisfy you. In fact, I will not offer you an explanation at all, because while that is what you want, it is not what you need.

Consider Job, whose story is recorded in the Bible. In a day, Job not only lost all his livestock but, much worse, all his children too—seven sons and three daughters. All gone in a tragic moment. But while he felt great loss and, like you, wondered about My role in that loss, I never answered the *why* question for Job. Explaining what I know would be like describing colors to a person born blind or a symphony to a person born deaf.[19]

I will give you something better than an explanation to help you endure the grief of losing one you loved. I will give you Myself. As it was for Job, any explanation will be inadequate, unacceptable, or incomprehensible. You need something more—you need Me.[20] Getting to know Me more intimately through your loss will prove to be much more of a comfort to you than a rational explanation.[21]

Instead of asking *why,* it is better to ask *what now.* Where do you turn for direction? Who helps you with the *what now* question? Do you know things about Me that bring you hope? Here's what the prophet Isaiah knew: "The righteous perish, and no one ponders it in his heart; devout men are taken away, and no one understands that the righteous are taken away to be spared from evil. Those who walk uprightly enter into peace; they find rest as they lie in death."[22]

The righteous are taken away to be spared from evil. That's the *why.* Here's the *what now:* All who love Me in this life enter into peace and find rest with Me in the next. Only a God who loves you can hold you tightly to Himself and help you as you grieve. Won't you let Me comfort you by becoming more intimate with Me and learning *what now?*

As King David said, "Even though I walk through the valley of the shadow of death, I will fear no evil, for you are with me; your rod and your staff, they comfort me."[23] Being with Me is the *what now.*

YOUR QUESTION

3) Why do You allow hunger?

GOD'S ANSWER

If you have read the beginning of the Bible, you know that I planted a perfect garden in Eden and "made all kinds of trees grow out of the ground—trees that were pleasing to the eye and good for food."[24] My garden was amply watered and got plenty of sunshine. Hunger was never a worry for Adam and Eve. I provided all that My creation needed to flourish. I told them they were free to eat of any tree of the Garden of Eden except one, the tree of the knowledge of good and evil. I even warned them that if they ate of that tree, they would experience more than hunger; they would experience death.[25]

Today, people meet and talk about the problem of hunger, but it still persists. There has been some progress and aid given, but the number of people in extreme poverty has increased.[26] While there is lots of talk, there is little done to address the problem. You ask Me, "Why do You allow hunger?" That's a legitimate question. Once you understand the cause, I'll ask you the same thing. Remember, I created the world with plenty to eat.

There are several causes for hunger in your world, but the chief one is poverty. Many poor people are hungry. There are 1.2 billion poor people in developing countries who live on one dollar a day or less.[27] But hunger is not only the result of poverty; it is also a cause of poverty. Some hungry people can't be productive because of low levels of energy and mental impairment. Until something is done to lessen poverty in the developing world, there is little people can do to eradicate hunger.

Many great obstacles to eradicating world hunger are political. I don't see people in rich countries doing much about it. Did you know that the world produces enough food to feed everyone? Right now, world agriculture produces 17 percent more calories per person daily than it did thirty years ago, despite a 70 percent population increase. This is enough to provide everyone in the world with at least 2,720 kilocalories (kcal) per person per day. People do not have to starve. The problem is distribution, not production. If people were not so selfish, if they weren't so belligerent toward one another, if there weren't such deep divisions in the world caused by the attitudes that arise from sinful hearts, feeding the world would not be a problem.

So, you ask Me why I allow people to starve. I have given you sufficient land to grow enough food to feed the world. I have given you machinery, technology, genetic research, and man power to get the job done. I have provided sufficient food for every person in the world to have enough to eat. I am not the one allowing people to starve. The world has all it needs to end this problem. Therefore, why do *you* allow hunger?

Notes

1. Genesis 1:4, 10, 12, 18, 25, 31. The word "very" is the Hebrew *meh-odé*. It means to a great degree, exceedingly, and abundantly. To gain some perspective on the meaning of the word, notice that it is used frequently in the Bible. God did not simply make Abram a rich man, He made him *very* rich (Genesis 13:2; 24:35). When God described the particular sin of the men of Sodom, He did not say homosexuality and sodomy were wicked; He said they were *"exceedingly* wicked and sinful against the Lord" (Genesis 13:13; 18:20 NKJV). God promised that the descendants of Abram would not just be plentiful, but that He would *greatly* increase the number of his descendants (Genesis 17:2). As He would do for Abraham through Isaac, so, too, He would do for Ishmael (Genesis 17:20). In each case, the emphasis is on excessiveness. When God viewed His creation, it wasn't just good. It was excessively good. He wasn't just pleased; He was elated.

2. Genesis 4:8.

3. Genesis 4:9, 19; 14:1–2; 19:5; 26:1; 27:15–17.

4. 2 Corinthians 11:23–27. The Bible does not record when Paul was beaten by the Jews with thirty-nine lashes. It records two occasions when he was beaten with rods, once at Philippi (Acts 16:22) and once at Jerusalem (Acts 21:32), but we don't know the third occasion. We know the incident when he was stoned; it was at Lystra (Acts 14:19). But the locations of other horrible events are not specifically recorded.

5. 2 Corinthians 12:7–10.

6. Psalm 34:18.

7. Matthew 10:29–31.

8. John 16:33.

9. Compare Genesis 1:26–28 with Psalm 8.

10. Genesis 3:17–19; Isaiah 11:6–9 and chapter 35; Romans 8:19–25.

11. 1 Thessalonians 4:13–14 CEV.

12. Romans 8:18.

13. Genesis 50:20.

14. Mark 15:34.

15. 2 Corinthians 5:21; 1 Timothy 2:5–6.

16. Genesis 2:17; 3:19; 5:5.

17. Romans 5:12.

18. Romans 1:18–21; 15:13; 1 Thessalonians 4:13–17; 1 Peter 1:3–7; 1 John 3:1–3.

19. Philip Yancey, *Disappointment with God* (Grand Rapids: Zondervan, 1988), 193.

20. 2 Corinthians 4:16–18; 5:1–9; Colossians 1:22. Frederick Buechner, in his book *Wishful Thinking*, notes, "God doesn't explain. He explodes. He asks Job who he thinks he is anyway. He says that to try to explain the kind of things Job wants explained would be like trying to explain Einstein to a little-neck clam . . . God doesn't reveal his grand design. He reveals himself." Frederick Buechner, *Wishful Thinking: A Theological ABC* (New York: Harper & Row, 1973), 46.

21. Nancy Guthrie explains, "God . . . doesn't reveal his master plan. Instead, he reveals himself, and in the midst of his awesome presence, Job's questions are not answered—they simply disappear (Job 40:1–5).

In his response, God does not explain suffering or how to avoid suffering. Suffering is a mystery . . . and Job comes to respect the mystery. Job comes to understand that because he knows who God is, he can accept what God gives—even when he doesn't understand it." *Holding on to Hope: A pathway through suffering to the heart of God* (Wheaton: Tyndale, 2002), 80.

22. Isaiah 57:1–2; Psalm 34:18.

23. Psalm 23:4.

24. Genesis 2:9.

25. Genesis 2:17.

26. www.worldhunger.org/articles/africa/ethiopiastarvation.htm. In 2002, conferences on hunger abounded: the World Food Conference, the World Summit on Sustainable Development held in South Africa, and the International Conference on Sustainable Development held in Monterrey, Mexico. There is no question that world hunger is one of the major challenges humanity faces in the twenty-first century. In 2002, hunger became widespread in Africa, with people at risk of famine increasing from several million to fifty million.

27. Of the 1.2 billion poor people in developing countries, 780 million suffer from chronic hunger. That means their daily intake of calories is insufficient for them to be healthy and lead a normal, active life. According to the Food and Agriculture Organization, in sub-Saharan Africa, there were fifty-eight million more poor people in 1999 than in 1990. See: http://www.worldhunger.org/articles/Learn/world%20hunger%20facts%202002.htm.

CHAPTER EIGHT

About My Life

BARNA PROFILE

Five percent of adults had questions that were related to specific incidents in their lives. Because the topics were unique to the respondents, there were a range of concerns: financial troubles, involvement in accidents, inability to have children, parents' divorce, life changes, handicapped children, unloving parents, career choices, and many others. Those with questions about their lives were more likely to not currently be married or to have had a divorce. Typical questions included:

1) **Why is my life messed up?**

2) **Have I been a good parent?**

3) **Why haven't You given me a companion?**

YOUR QUESTION

1) Why is my life messed up?

GOD'S ANSWER

Many people ask Me this question. They say, "I've tried to do the right thing and yet my life is so messed up. Why?" There are things common to humanity that have adverse effects.

First, not all the challenges you face in life are of your own making. Don't blame yourself for other people's sins. A person who had an abusive father did not make him that way. Each person is accountable for his own actions. You are not in control over all of the circumstances of your life or the people in it.

But let us reason together. Sometimes it is your fault. You are not the sole perpetuator of problems in your life, but you are a contributor. That's the case when you make bad choices. Failure to control your mind and body always leads to disappointment.[1] Failure to curb appetites can lead to bad choices, like getting into excessive debt or abusing the body with food, drugs, or alcohol. The most common bad choices involve other people. I see individuals blurring the lines between lust and love, and, while they are seeking love, they settle for lust. People who join their bodies, souls, and spirits together through sexual intercourse outside of marriage are setting themselves up for the excruciating pain of separation once the affair is over. I want people to live in ways that bring glory and honor to Me. Whatever you do, do it in a way that brings Me glory. I want us to share closeness that comes from deep knowledge of one another.

Often people make bad choices because they believe all sorts of falsehoods. They actually reverse the truth, calling black, white, and calling up, down. I warned the prophet Isaiah about this: "Woe to those who call evil good and good evil, who put darkness for light and light for darkness, who put bitter for sweet and sweet for bitter."[2] It's easy to be fooled when the truth is distorted, even if you know better. All you need is someone saying darkness is light long enough for you to begin to believe it. While purity and modesty were once considered good by your society, they are becoming less and less valued. But My standards do not change. What have changed are the attitudes of people who are willing to call good, evil, and call evil, good.

Your life is messed up because the world you live in is messed up. You are impacted by it and you contribute to it. "Just as sin entered the world through one man (Adam), and death through sin, and in this way death came to all men, because all sinned."[3] Your world is permeated by sin. Now people face the challenge of cleaning up their lives.

If you want to see a turnaround in your life, do not continue in patterns of poor life choices. They are not set in concrete, and I can help you change. However, you need My help, and I am more than willing to give it to you. Here are three things you can do.

First, face the facts. Be real. Don't tell Me your life is messed up and then go on living as if it weren't so bad. If you want to change, admit it. Tell Me about it. Be honest. Face the reality that your life won't get better by doing the same things you've done in the past.

Second, take initiative. Don't just sit back and let bad things happen to you. Don't let your friends' bad choices continue to influence your life and don't keep blaming them, or Me, for your life being the way it is. Take responsibility for how you live instead of blaming others. You must admit where and how you are the source of the problems in your life.

Third, trust Me. I can change you. I can straighten up the mess in your life. I can forgive you for what you've done to yourself and others. Here's what John preached as good news to hold on to: "If we confess our sins, he (that's Me, God) is faithful and just and will forgive us our sins and purify us from all unrighteousness."[4] Flee from your sins and claim forgiveness.

I am a Father, your heavenly Father. Good fathers, like Me, want what is best for our children and it pains us when we see them messing up their lives. But like the good father in the story of the prodigal son, I am eager for you to come back to Me. Read that wonderful story in the Bible, found in Luke 15:11–32. Do what that prodigal did when he messed up his life, and I'll do what his father did when he came home to him. I am waiting for you.

YOUR QUESTION

2) Have I been a good parent?

GOD'S ANSWER

You can determine the answer to this question if you have the right criteria by which to evaluate your parenting. I'll remind you what the Bible says about it, and then you'll know whether or not you've been a good parent. Good parents have certain qualities in common.

Children learn love and respect from those they love and respect. If your kids see the love you have for Me, for each other, and for them, they will copy and reciprocate it.[5] Children need to see love, feel love, and experience love, not just be told "I love you." They need "hands-on" love. They also need to see moms and dads in love with each other. "Husbands, love your wives and do not be harsh with them."[6]

"Love the LORD your God with all your heart and with all your soul and with all your strength. These commandments that I give you today are to be upon your hearts. Impress them on your children. Talk about them when you sit at home and when you walk along the road, when you lie down and when you get up. Tie them as symbols on your hands and bind them on your foreheads. Write them on the doorframes of your houses and on your gates."[7] Love is like a good virus; let your kids catch it.

Good parenting requires honesty. There is no bigger child complaint, especially among teenagers, than phony parents. Children want parents to say, do, and live the truth.[8] You ought not shade the truth from your children because you will lose their trust. I want your children to "see your good deeds and glorify God."[9]

Good parenting requires physical, emotional, and spiritual protection. You and your children need spiritual protection most of all. Jesus said, "No one can enter a strong man's house and carry off his possessions unless he first ties up the strong man. Then he can rob his house."[10] Fathers, this is primarily your responsibility. More robbers enter your house through the Internet and other media than come through your front door. Good parents set guidelines and monitor their children's habits. They have discussions with their children about what is good and is evil.

Good parenting means establishing well-defined and understood boundaries. The happiest and most secure children are those who know what the limits are. But be prepared; they will surely test those limits. Many teens who are told their curfew is 11:00 P.M. will come home at 11:10 P.M. What will you do? Will you let them get away with it, or will you make the curfew ten minutes earlier next time? If your child throws a fit and gets his way, you can be sure you'll see more fits because he has learned that whining works. Are your rules reasonable, clear, and enforceable?

Good parenting means you identify and instill My values in your children. If you don't, there's someone waiting at school, the mall, or the playground, quite willing to share his values with your child. It is both your right and responsibility as parents to talk to your kids about the things that are important.

Good parenting also means good mentoring. When Jesus said, "I am the good shepherd," He was defining Himself as the model to follow.[11] Your children need to see in you a kind, considerate, faithful, and true model of what they need to become. To accomplish this requires consistency in your emotions, in enforcing restrictions, and in demonstrating love in all things.

There's much more, of course. The book of Proverbs is a treasure trove of wisdom about raising children. And don't worry about not being perfect. Just seek Me and ask for My help every day in raising your children. Read what I've told you in My Word. And enjoy being a parent!

YOUR QUESTION

3) Why haven't You given me a companion?

GOD'S ANSWER

People are single for different reasons. And if the single population in your country formed their own country, they would make up the twelfth largest nation in the world. Some of you are single because you have never married, some are now divorced, and some have become a widow or widower.[12]

Many people are unhappy about being single. Your society pushes people to find a mate and expects singles to feel dissatisfied. While some say your life is lacking without a mate, I do not see it that way and neither should you.

How are you to respond to people whose friendship discourages you as a single? Like Job you want to shout, "miserable comforters are you all!"[13] More important, how do you respond to your own feelings of loneliness? If you constantly pine away for companionship, little will change your condition. But if you are willing to step back from your life, look at it from a different perspective, you'll discover joy and fulfillment in the single life.[14]

People have responded to their marital status in different ways. Some have quietly accepted singleness as their lot in life, gone back to bed, and pulled the covers over their head. Others have boastfully promoted the virtues of the single life, expressing sympathy for married people.

Have you ever received a gift that, at first, you didn't like? You couldn't figure out how you would ever use it. Singleness is like that. The apostle Paul counsels the believers at Corinth not to question being unmarried or seek to be released from their marital status because both are from Me. He says, "I wish that all men were as I am. But each man has his own gift from God; one has this gift, another has that."[15] For Paul, the real issue is not his marital status but rather choosing to exercise his gift of singleness in a way that brings glory to Me and joy to him. His question is not "What do I want for myself?" but it is rather "What does God want for me?" Those who come to appreciate singleness as much as marriage begin to look for ways to use their gift instead of coveting the gift of another.

The reason some have the gift of marriage and others have the gift of singleness is the same reason some have the gift of teaching and others have the gift of administration. In his discussion of spiritual gifts, the apostle Paul used the analogy of a body to highlight the diversity of gifts given to My people. The physical body needs hands, a nose, feet, eyes, and ears, etc. "God has arranged the parts in the body, every one of them, just as he wanted them to be."[16] What a grotesque body it would be if each part randomly chose where it would fit. This is also true for marital status and spiritual gifts. Some in the body of Christ (the family of Christians) are married and others are not. Your personal contribution to the body of Christ can be affected by your marital status.

Singleness opens doors to service that married people can never go through. My Son said, "For some are eunuchs because they were born that way; others were made that way by men; and others have renounced marriage because of the kingdom of heaven."[17] I can work through your life in ways I cannot work with those who are married. I have used many single people for great good, like Mary, Martha, and Lazarus.

Philip the Evangelist was blessed with four unmarried daughters who engaged in a successful and fruitful prophetic ministry.[18] And My own Son was never married but gladly gave Himself to the mission I had for Him. My Son said to Me, "Not my will, but yours be done."[19] An eternal perspective enables people to enjoy contributing to the family and Kingdom of God in whatever capacity they serve.[20]

While the world tries to squeeze you into its mold and attempts to pair you up and marry you off, remember that I have never viewed singleness as a bad thing. When I said, "It is not good for the man to be alone,"[21] I expressed the need for womanhood. If men were left alone, there would be no offspring. I gave equal value to women and men. But being unmarried has never been wrong. In his classic treatment of marriage, Paul repeated three times that it is good to remain unmarried.[22]

Many men and women marry to relieve a societal stigma of singleness, and in doing so, they doom themselves to misery. Ask yourself whether you are better off single or trapped in a love-lacking marriage. Self-centeredness often rears its ugly head among married couples once the honeymoon stage is over. Many problems surface from mismatched couples. How is singleness not preferable to marriage outside of My will?

So, why haven't I given you a companion? You may not appreciate or understand My reasons in your earthly lifetime, but if you want to enjoy your life and make something of it that counts for eternity, drain yourself of self-pity and begin to see your singleness with divine purpose. What could be better than discovering the highest calling for your life? I want you to have ultimate joy, and sometimes that means walking single file.

Notes

1. 1 Thessalonians 4:3–8.

2. Isaiah 5:20.

3. Romans 5:12.

4. 1 John 1:9.

5. Ecclesiastes 12:13; John 13:14–17; 1 Timothy 1:16; Titus 2:1–8; 1 Peter 5:2–4.

6. Ephesians 5:25; Colossians 3:19.

7. Deuteronomy 6:5–9; Luke 10:27.

8. Romans 12:17; 2 Corinthians 8:21; Philippians 4:8.

9. 1 Peter 2:12.

10. Mark 3:27.

11. John 10:11.

12. Approximately 60 percent of American singles have never been married. God truly understands the single life. He is God the Father, but there is no God the Mother. In fact, God is the original single parent. The wholeness God finds in Himself, and in His equals—God the Son and God the Spirit—is the model for singles everywhere to find their own wholeness.

    Approximately 25 percent of the American singles population is divorced. One-sixth of all American singles are widows or widowers. A helpful analysis of singles in America has been compiled by Barna Research. You may access this information online at www.barna.org. Look at Recent Barna Updates and click on "View entire list." The information on singles in America is contained in the March 11, 2002 update entitled, "A Revealing Look at Three Unique Single Adult Populations." Or get the full story in George Barna's book *Single Focus* (Ventura, Calif.: Gospel Light, 2003).

13. Job 16:2.

14. Clinical psychologist Joel Rachelson calls this being a "Conscious Single," taking a step back in your awareness of yourself, or of yourself with others, or of yourself in relationship to tasks, objects, the world, etc. It is having the capacity to self-observe, not to self-pity. See: http://www.innerself.com/Relationships/conscioussingle.htm. Psychotherapist Maryam Jorjani has written a book entitled, *What's*

Wrong with Being Single? (New York: Omid Publishing, 2000) that is a challenge to single people to throw off the shackles of self-pity and celebrate the benefits of singleness.

15. 1 Corinthians 7:7.

16. 1 Corinthians 12:18.

17. Matthew 19:12.

18. Acts 21:8–9.

19. Luke 22:42.

20. Henrietta C. Mears was one of the great Bible teachers of the twentieth century. While Christian Education Director at First Presbyterian Church of Hollywood, she built one of the largest Sunday schools in the world and wrote curriculum that was in such high demand that to publish it she founded Gospel Light in 1933. The late Richard C. Halverson, Chaplain of the U.S. Senate and Bill Bright, founder of Campus Crusade for Christ, were among her students. Nancy Leigh DeMoss admired the life and work of Henrietta Mears and discovered singleness as her gift too. She especially connects with the desires and goals of single women in her books, radio talks, and personal appearances.

21. Genesis 2:18.

22. 1 Corinthians 7:1, 8, 26.

Personal Request

BARNA PROFILE

This category was similar to the previous one in that the questions posed were unique and diverse. However, these questions indicated some type of request of God. Four percent of adults had such requests. Those with this kind of personal request of God were likely to be a female or an Elder. Typical questions included:

1) Can You give people in this world a better life?

2) Can You help me get a job?

3) Can You help me be a better person?

4) Can You give me strength to deal with stuff happening in this world?

YOUR QUESTION

1) Can You give people in this world a better life?

GOD'S ANSWER

I certainly can give you a better life, and I am more willing to provide it than you are willing to receive it. The life I originally created for you is much better than what you are experiencing now. Once humans chose to know (and live) good and evil, they began sinning, and the quality of life took a significant downfall.[1] It was My intent for you to have a better life. "I know the plans I have for you . . . plans to prosper you and not to harm you, plans to give you hope and a future."[2]

Most people don't know what a better life is. Even though I've told them in My Book how to have a better life, people still don't seem to know where to find it. Men and women try to buy a better life by purchasing products to decrease hair loss and wrinkles and increase muscle mass and sexual drive. All this world has to offer still leaves people with something missing.

People are looking for a better life in all the wrong places. Many have turned to quality-of-life pharmacology, wanting science to produce miracle drugs and products.[3] Some of these products help the physical body, but they offer little to feed and nourish the soul.

Some people have looked for a better life through mere spirituality. Certain groups believe that many "higher states of existence" are available to their members.[4] They take steps to chart an upward course of improvement. Still, so many do not take into account what I have to say about a better life.

In the Bible I call a better life "abundant life." Listen to what My Son said: "I have come that they may have life, and have it to the full."[5] What did He mean? How can you have a better life right now?

A better life is not one filled with more money, toys, social events, or anything else. The better life you are looking for is not found in being slimmer or healthier or having larger this or smaller that. The better life you need is found in better relationships, especially a deeper relationship with Me.[6] The closer you are to Me, your Creator, the better your life will be for all eternity.

I offer a better life to you, not through pharmacology, Scientology, or psychology—not through reconstruction or gradation, but through redemption. When Jesus died for you on Calvary's cross, it wasn't only to pay the penalty for your sin and redeem you from its guilt and punishment. It was to restore your relationship with Me, a relationship severed by disobedience and sin. Jesus' death wasn't just to give His life *for* you; it was to give His life *to* you as well. The life He wants to give you now, right where you are, is the life that allows Him to work in you and through your actions.

Can I give people in this world a better life? Yes, both in the future and right now. It's a matter of placing your faith in the Son of God as the One who met every requirement I had for your redemption. Receiving the life Jesus offers doesn't guarantee you fun or riches, but it does bring you joy and better things than you can imagine.

YOUR QUESTION

2) Can You help me get a job?

GOD'S ANSWER

I've already given you a job. Your job is to be a follower of the Savior, Jesus Christ. You are to "go and make disciples of all nations."[7] I know that's not the kind of job you were talking about, and I'll answer your question. But before I do, I want you to think about what I told you. I have already given you a job—a job with guaranteed lifetime employment, no layoffs, no downsizings, and no cutbacks. And it's the most important job you will ever have. You dare not dismiss this important work simply to find employment.

You are looking for a job that brings home a paycheck. And that is the way life is—people work to provide themselves with food and shelter. David was a shepherd. Paul was a tentmaker. William Carey was a shoemaker. But each of these people saw their vocation as a means to a greater end. David used his shepherding skills as king of Israel, leading them during turbulent years. Paul used his trade as a tentmaker to provide food and clothing, but he was involved in a much greater endeavor.[8] While William Carey repaired shoes, he learned Latin, Greek, Hebrew, French, and Dutch. In his teenage years he could read the Bible in six languages. Little wonder he became the father of modern missions. He saw his work as a cobbler as a means to a much greater end.

Each of these people recognized that their vocation was a way to keep the body and soul together while they were about their real business—the business of being a witness and servant of the Lord Jesus. Don't ever confuse employment with your life's work. I will provide employment for you too. Be diligent in seeking it, but be abundantly more diligent in seeking Me.[9] Your more important "work" is belonging to My family, helping others into the family, and letting My righteousness be exhibited through your life.

While looking for employment, you need to trust Me. Bring your needs to Me. Bring them often. If you need a job, ask Me for one. Many times "you do not have, because you do not ask God."[10] Also, be willing to put effort into a job search. Not all jobs fall into your lap. You have to go after a job as you would go after anything worthwhile.

You ought not think that a certain job "is not good enough." I don't care what haughty people think about jobs and status. You can do your work honorably, whether it is cleaning, maintenance, truck driving, business, or something else. What is available may not be your first choice, but it may be the solution to your current problem. Remember, one of the principles in My Book is the reward of the faithful. In Jesus' parable of the talents, the master said to his servant who did the little things that his master gave him to do, "Well done, good and faithful servant! You have been faithful with a few things; I will put you in charge of many things."[11]

Be sure you use the resources available to you in searching for a job. I have given you gifts and talents that you can use in a variety of places. Government agencies help the unemployed, as I have ordained them to help and direct the people. Don't be too proud to use agencies, listings, and your mouth; you can ask others to let you know if they hear of work available, and you can inquire of managers who are able to hire you. Pray about opportunities that come your way.

Finally, you need to see work the right way. It is one of My gifts to you. I have promised that good, hard work will bring the rewards of satisfaction, fulfillment, and payment. In fact, your attitude toward work is so important that the Bible commands the believers in Thessalonica to withdraw from those people who are not seeking to pull their own weight. "If a man will not work, he shall not eat."[12] Of course, there are times when a person who cannot find work is unemployed. The members of My family and government ought to help. But Paul warned the Thessalonians not to support the lazy, the indigent, and those who have the opportunity to work but not the desire. Laziness is not My plan for you. Make sure it is not your plan for you.

I don't want you to give up when a job does not come your way quickly. Start with prayer and then act. Remember, Jesus told His disciples stories and gave examples to show them that they should always pray and not give up.[13] That's what you should do too. I'll work behind the scenes as you look for work and look to Me.

YOUR QUESTION

3) Can You help me be a better person?

GOD'S ANSWER

I can definitely help you be a better person. But *better* is a value judgment. Better than what? How will you know when you are better? More importantly, why do you want to be a better person? What will being a better person get you? Certainly not salvation. Becoming a better person won't get you to heaven.

A rich young man came to Jesus and wanted to earn eternal life. He said that he had kept all the commandments of My law, but he somehow sensed he still wasn't good enough. He asked Jesus what he still lacked. Jesus shocked the rich young man by giving him a challenge, knowing that this man was unwilling to put God before his earthly wealth. Jesus said to the rich man, "If you want to be perfect, go, sell your possessions and give to the poor, and you will have treasure in heaven. Then come, follow me." That was too much for the man. He wanted to be better, but not at that price. "When the young man heard this, he went away sad, because he had great wealth."[14] What Jesus wanted this man to understand was that no matter how good a person becomes, he can't become good enough to merit heaven. Salvation is the free gift of My grace. This gift has to be accepted because you can never become good enough.[15] So if you thought that becoming a better person would make you good enough for Me to welcome you into My heaven, think again.

But once you are aware that becoming better isn't what saves your soul, the question of becoming a better person is quite legitimate. What is it that makes you a better you? Better people have better character.

Character is who you are, not just how you think or behave. How you think and act only *reflect* your character. Consider My servant D. L. Moody. He said, "Character is what you are in the dark." It is what you are when no one else is looking. You become a better person when you have a better character.

So where will you learn character traits that make you a better person? I've already identified them in My Book. If you want your character to become better, reflect My character. When you express faith in My Son as Savior, I'll help you become a better person. Here are some important character traits that are identified in My Word.

Love. To be enjoyed, love must be demonstrated. When you imitate the same self-sacrificing love that My Son exhibited when He died for you, you'll reflect love in action. Good character demands loving responses to people, even to those who do not reciprocate your love.[16]

Joy. Being a person of joyful disposition arises from something deep in your character; it is not just a temporary feeling. True joy doesn't depend on your circumstances. It is an expression of a renewed, repaired, rejoicing, and right relationship with Me. Joy expresses itself even in the dark times of life.

Peace. Being at peace with others, yourself, and Me is proof of godly character. It is an inner quietness, even when the world is chaotic around you and when people hate you for no reason. It is My gift and defies human understanding.[17] Again, it is a state of being, not a mere feeling.

Patience. You have plenty of opportunities to demonstrate patience. You can refuse to lash out when you are provoked, whether you are at home, the office, or even in traffic. This kind of patience reflects My forbearance for those who continually flaunt their sin in My face.

Kindness. When you show people genuine kindness, you become a better person. I demonstrated kindness in providing My Son as your Savior. Now I want everyone who has experienced My kindness to imitate Me and pass it on to others.[18]

Goodness. I don't expect you to be perfect. You already know you cannot become good enough to enter heaven on your own merit, but you can become better than you are. Goodness resides in the heart more than the head. It is having a rightness about your soul, a righteousness that makes you want to help others, even when they do not deserve it. I give that kind of goodness.

Faithfulness. It grieves Me to see the lack of this quality in your world. Divorce is rampant because faithfulness isn't treasured anymore. Productivity is down because workers often are interested only in their paycheck and do not value an honest day's work. But a faithful character produces a faithful person. Faithful people are trustworthy and reliable, even when it's not easy for them to be so.[19]

Gentleness. This doesn't mean you have the weakness of an ant. It means you are considerate of others.[20] Husbands need to be more tender and gentle with their wives. And wives need to be more gentle with their husbands by refraining from quarreling and losing their tempers.

Self-control. This quality is less and less evident in your world. People won't control their eating, their drinking, their sexual desires, their spending, or anything else. Godly character reflects self-mastery, character that can say no to ungodliness and make it stick.[21] Learn to curb your appetites.

These are the character traits listed in Galatians 5:22–23. Take a good look at them. Which character traits best describe you? I'm pleased that you're interested in becoming a better person. Read My Word and follow where the good character qualities take you.

YOUR QUESTION

4) Can You give me strength to deal with stuff happening in the world?

GOD'S ANSWER

There are many terrible things happening in your world today, like famine, disease, terrorism, and divorce. People worry more than ever. These are tough times. They're dark times. How can you cope? I have the answer.

King David said, "Do not fret because of evil men."[22] The word "fret" means to be hot or burn, to be furious. Do not become furious with Me when you see things happening you can't explain. "Sinful people are happy for only a while."[23] If it seems like things are getting worse instead of better, it's because they are. "Evil men and imposters will go from bad to worse."[24] But don't lose heart. One day I will right all the wrongs and set things straight. "Will not the Judge of all the earth do right?"[25] If you remember that, you will have strength to deal with what is happening in the world today.

There's something else you need to be careful of. Do not be jealous of those who live ungodly lives. You see people who curse Me, deny My existence, and hate Me. These people seem to be "getting ahead" when you are not. Again David suggested that you not "be envious of those who do wrong."[26] Jealousy, if it doesn't kill you, will sour your life so badly that you'll wish you were dead.[27] Even if you love Me, you can be entangled by the snare of jealousy. Asaph, who wrote some wonderful poetry in praise of Me, admitted, "For I envied the arrogant when I saw the prosperity of the wicked."[28] But you need to draw upon My strength to defeat jealousy. If you don't, it can become a wedge between us that neither of us wants. Don't be jealous of sinners, but always honor Me. Then you will truly have hope for the future.[29]

I've told you two things you shouldn't do if you want My strength. Are there things you should do? Let David tell you. "Trust in the LORD and do good."[30] The king learned this lesson through experience. He had a lot of bad things happen in his life. One of his sons, Amnon, raped one of his daughters, Tamar.[31] Another son, Adonijah, tried to grab the throne when David was old and sick.[32] And David's favorite son, Absalom, not only killed Amnon but conspired to overthrow David and take the throne for himself.[33] To humiliate his father, Absalom even pitched a tent on the rooftop and, in public view of all, slept with David's concubines. From his early years of being shunned by his brothers to being hunted down by the jealous King Saul to later years of family disappointments, David saw much of life's dark side. Still he says, "Trust in the LORD and do good."

How can anyone say that? Did David have a good grasp on reality? He not only had a firm grasp on reality; he had a firm grasp on faith. He had learned the only thing that could help him handle trouble in his life was faith in Me. David didn't stay down when he got down because I raised his head in My strength.[34] He had learned to pray to Me, lean on Me, and trust Me for strength to deal with the circumstances of his life.[35]

When you can't explain what you see, don't get burned up at Me because I don't intervene when you think I should. Instead, trust Me and do the right thing. Have you noticed how many different people in the Bible have testified that I gave them strength when they needed it most? Moses said: "The LORD is my strength and my song; he has become my salvation."[36] David boasted: "It is God who arms me with strength."[37] Isaiah said of Me: "You will keep in perfect peace him whose mind is steadfast, because he trusts in you. Trust in the LORD forever, for the LORD, the LORD, is the Rock eternal."[38] Jeremiah called Me his strength and fortress, his refuge in times of distress.[39] Joel knew that "The LORD will be a refuge for his people, a stronghold for the people of Israel."[40] Habakkuk said: "The Sovereign LORD is my strength; he makes my feet like the feet of a deer, he enables me to go on the heights."[41] Paul realized he could do everything through Me who gave him strength.[42] And Peter encourages you, declaring: "And the God of all grace, who called you to his eternal glory in Christ, after you have suffered a little while, will himself restore you and make you strong, firm and steadfast."[43]

Don't miss what these people found. When things happen that are difficult to handle, let Me give you strength— My strength. Look to Me and My strength; seek My face always.[44] My strength is available to you. Ask for it.[45]

Notes

1. Genesis 1–3.

2. Jeremiah 29:11.

3. "Where all this technology is taking us is into a series of qualitative improvements in people's lives," said William Haseltine, head of Human Genomes Sciences, Inc. His company is in the vanguard of the new pharmacology.

4. The Church of Scientology believes this. Its founder, L. Ron Hubbard, provided a precise delineation of these states and taught his followers how they could gradually attain them.

5. John 10:10.

6. Leonard Syme, a professor of epidemiology at the University of California at Berkeley, did a study on the effects of relationships to death and disease. According to him, Japan is the number one nation in the world when it comes to health. And his findings indicated that it was because the Japanese people have strong relationships with family and therefore better health and a lower death rate. Quoted in Martin and Diedre Bobgan, *How to Counsel from Scripture* (Chicago: Moody, 1985), 18.

7. Matthew 28:19–20.

8. Acts 18:3.

9. Matthew 6:33.

10. James 4:2.

11. Matthew 25:23.

12. 2 Thessalonians 3:10.

13. Luke 18:1–8.

14. Matthew 19:16–30.

15. God's grace means that He deals favorably with us in response to our expression of faith in Jesus Christ as Savior. He does not deal with us as we deserve but graciously, as we do not deserve. Read about this undeserved favor in Romans 1:17; 3:19–28; 4:1–6; 5:1; Galatians 2:16; Ephesians 2:8–10.

16. 1 John 4:11.

17. John 15:18; Philippians 4:7; 1 Peter 4:12–19.

18. 2 Corinthians 6:6; Ephesians 5:1–2; Colossians 3:12.

19. Luke 16:10–12.

20. 1 Timothy 6:11–12.

21. Titus 2:11–14.

22. Psalm 37:1.

23. Job 20:5 CEV.

24. 2 Timothy 3:13.

25. Genesis 18:25.

26. Psalm 37:1.

27. Proverbs 14:30.

28. Psalm 73:3.

29. Proverbs 23:17–18 CEV.

30. Psalm 37:3.

31. 2 Samuel 13:1–22.

32. 1 Kings 1.

33. 2 Samuel 13:23–39; 15–18.

34. Psalm 3:1–5; 4:8.

35. Psalm 18:1–3.

36. Exodus 15:2.

37. 2 Samuel 22:33.

38. Isaiah 26:3–4.

39. Jeremiah 16:19.

40. Joel 3:16.

41. Habakkuk 3:19.

42. Philippians 4:13.

43. 1 Peter 5:10.

44. 1 Chronicles 16:11; Psalm 105:4.

45. James 4:2.

Faith & Spirituality

BARNA PROFILE

Four percent of adults had questions related to their faith or to spiritual matters. Those with spiritual or faith-related questions were more likely to: consider themselves to have an active faith; have attended a church worship service in the past week; or reside in the West. Typical questions included:

1) Am I living my life in a way that pleases You?

2) When are You (Jesus) coming back?

3) How can I serve You better?

YOUR QUESTION

1) Am I living my life in a way that pleases You?

GOD'S ANSWER

I am pleased that you ask this question. How you live is very important to Me. Fathers always want their children to live in ways that please them.

I've already said some things in My Book about pleasing Me. King David asked, "Who may ascend the hill of the LORD? Who may stand in his holy place?" He answered his own question: "He who has clean hands and a pure heart."[1] Do you know the only One who is completely pure in thought, word, and deed? My Son, Jesus Christ, is the only One. Yet He gives His righteousness to sinners. Your heart and the works of your hands are clean and pure as Christ lives through you.

I enjoy it when you praise My goodness in word and song and glorify Me with thanksgiving. There is nothing sweeter than people singing in gratitude for their salvation. That's what David said in Psalm 69:30–31: "I will praise God's name in song and glorify him with thanksgiving. This will please the LORD more than an ox, more than a bull with its horns and hoofs."[2] David knew that I would be more pleased with his genuine praise than a sacrifice or offering.

Allow your mind and heart to be controlled by My Holy Spirit. It's easy for your mind to wander. Sinful temptations pop up regularly. If you flee from them, that pleases Me. "The mind of sinful man is death, but the mind controlled by the Spirit is life and peace; the sinful mind is hostile to God.

It does not submit to God's law, nor can it do so. Those controlled by the sinful nature cannot please God."[3]

A verse in the book of Hebrews addresses what is needed to please Me. Hebrews 11:6: "And without faith it is impossible to please God, because anyone who comes to him must believe that he exists and that he rewards those who earnestly seek him." When you trust Me and have faith in My existence, even if you don't understand what's going on in your life and in the world, that pleases Me.

There are other ways too. The apostle Paul wrote a letter to the Thessalonians instructing them how to live a life that pleases Me.[4] If you take a close look at this letter, even at just the first chapter, you'll see many things that are a part of this way of living.[5] In case you were wondering, living your life in a way that pleases Me is a reward in itself, and it shows that you have joined the army of the saved and redeemed to make a difference in your world.[6] While those who please Me will still endure persecution and trials, there will be times when I will make even your enemies be at peace with you.[7] Adopting a lifestyle that pleases Me is what is best for you.

YOUR QUESTION

2) When are You (Jesus) coming back?

GOD'S ANSWER

The one definitive statement in the Bible about when Jesus will return is that you don't know when He will return.

The disciples followed Jesus for three years, watched His miracles, and listened to His teaching. They heard Him say things about His kingdom.[8] Some people interpreted His words to mean that He would be establishing an earthly kingdom.[9] But then came the crucifixion. Their hopes were dashed. Everything they believed was challenged. They likely would have been ruined if Sunday morning hadn't come. Jesus rose from the dead and showed Himself alive to His disciples. Forty days later as He was about to return to heaven, His disciples asked, "Lord, are you at this time going to restore the kingdom to Israel?"[10] That's when He made this definitive statement about His return: "It is not for you to know the times or dates the Father has set by his own authority." There are some things I don't tell you, and when Jesus is going to return is one of them.[11]

I have good reasons for not revealing the exact time of My Son's return. I want you to anticipate His return, and if people knew when it would happen, that would dissipate the anticipation. Some would not feel accountable for their actions and plan a lifetime of godless living until right before He came. But that would only draw their hearts farther away from Me, perhaps for all eternity. Upon informing His disciples, "No one knows about that day or hour," Jesus admonished them, "Be on guard! Be alert!"[12] You need that "perhaps today" dimension to Jesus' return to prompt godly living and remind you that this world isn't all there is.

The other side of not living godlessly is living in holiness. In the days approaching the Lord's coming to you, I want you to lead lives of purity. As John said: "Dear friends, now we are children of God, and what we will be has not yet been made known. But we know that when he appears, we shall be like him, for we shall see him as he is. Everyone who has this hope in him purifies himself, just as he is pure."[13] Day by day you can become more like My Son, and when you see Him you will no longer be able to sin.

However, because I choose not to reveal the exact time of My Son's return does not mean you can't benefit from some informed observations. There are numerous references in the Bible that provide clues to the return of the Lord. Some things that need to happen are: 1) the reconstitution of the nation Israel, 2) the return of Jerusalem to Israel, and 3) the rapid increase in knowledge, the pervasiveness of godlessness, and the breakdown of families and societies. When you see these signs, you will know that the end is near.

My prophets prophesied that the nation Israel, dispersed throughout the world after they were carried off into captivity, would one day return to the Holy Land and become a nation again.[14] Israel lost its nationhood more than twenty six hundred years ago, but the Bible predicted that the fig tree, Israel, would bud again.[15] That budding took place in 1948 when, against all odds, God's chosen people returned to their homeland and established the modern state of Israel. That should encourage you that Jesus is coming soon.

The Bible also predicted that Jerusalem, the city of God, would be trampled under the feet of Gentile nations. This occurred during those hundreds of years when the Jews were scattered to other parts of the world. The Jewish people returned in 1948 to establish their nation, but their capital was still under the control of the British, the Jordanians, and others. Then, for just six days in 1967, a war was fought between Israel and her Arab neighbors, and Jerusalem came under Jewish control again. That's another reason to believe that Jesus is coming soon.

A third important sign will be a treaty signed between

Israel and the Antichrist. Although you don't know the identity of this person, you have learned that he will rule over ten European nations that correspond to what was the ancient Roman Empire. The Bible indicates he will cut a deal with Israel for peace.[16] This pact is for seven years, but in the middle of those years he will break the pact by a military assault on Jerusalem.[17] This attack occurs during the greatest period of tribulation the world has ever seen. Before any of this takes place, however, the body of Christ, the universal church as a whole, is removed from the earth in the Rapture. So, if being caught up in the air with Christ is imminent, can the appearance of the Antichrist be far behind?

Don't think you can calculate the future based on these and other prophecies. Many have tried and failed and embarrassed themselves. That is another reason why I choose not to answer your question directly.

Is there anything, then, a person can say for sure about the Lord's return? Yes. It's going to happen, just as He said. Jesus is coming back. He promised, "I am going there to prepare a place for you. And if I go and prepare a place for you, I will come back and take you to be with me that you also may be where I am."[18] You can trust Jesus because He always keeps His promises.

YOUR QUESTION

3) How can I serve You better?

GOD'S ANSWER

When people want to serve Me better, they often do one of the following: study and attend classes to get more education, attend a weekend seminar on the new methods of ministry, read a book on service, or hurry off to a session conducted by a popular leader. Can you learn to serve Me better by doing these things? Yes. But *will* you serve Me better? Sometimes yes and sometimes no. These are not the secrets to service. The secrets to serving Me better are demonstrated by a lowly woman who wanted to serve her Lord more than anything. Her story is recorded in Mark chapter 14.

It was just before His crucifixion and resurrection. Jesus was in Jerusalem at the house of Simon. One of the women there, Mary, was overcome in her adoration for the Lord, and she wanted to do something to demonstrate her love. She had an alabaster jar of very expensive perfume with her. It was made from pure nard, an aromatic extract from a root in India and Tibet. It was expensive because it had to be brought to that land by elephants and camels. She opened the jar and poured the perfume on Jesus' head. In doing so, she gave you a great example of how you can serve Me better. Here are the lessons you should learn.

First, she gave her very best to the Savior. If you want to serve well, you must give the very best you have. I am not impressed with those who give Me what is left over or what no one else wants. In the days of the prophet Malachi, people sacrificed to Me animals that were blind, crippled, or diseased. I told them, "Try offering them to your governor! Would he be pleased with you?"[19] Of course not. If another person would not be pleased with less than your best, why do you think I would? I deserve your very best.

Second, Mary teaches you that you reap what you sow. It's a law of agriculture: "Whoever sows sparingly will also reap sparingly, and whoever sows generously will also reap generously."[20] She did not sprinkle a little of the precious perfume on Jesus' head; she poured the contents of the whole jar on Him. She sowed generously, so she will reap generously. If you want to reap generous rewards in the future, you have to be generous in your service now.

The next lesson Mary teaches you is one of the hardest to learn. No sooner had she generously offered this perfume to her Lord than were her motives falsely judged. Remember this: When you are serving Me, even the purest motivation can be misunderstood. Don't let your critics get you down. You can spot a jealous person by the way he criticizes success.

Here's a very important lesson for anyone who wants to serve Me better: Do what you can, not what you dream. It's all right to dream, but it is better to get things done. When Mary was criticized, Jesus responded to her critics, saying, "She did what she could." Mary was not a disciple or an apostle. She couldn't preach, couldn't become a missionary in a far-off land, but she could show her love for her Savior. She did what she could. I am much more interested in you doing what you can today to serve Me than dreaming of big things you'll do someday.

Jesus closed the conversation about this woman with these words: "I tell you the truth, wherever the gospel is preached throughout the world, what she has done will also be told, in memory of her." Do you want to serve Me better? Then let Me make a name for you; don't make it your goal to make a name for yourself.

In nineteenth-century Yorkshire, England, two sons were born into a family named Taylor. The older set out to make a name for himself. He entered Parliament. The younger son chose to give his life to Me and serve Me all the days of his life. Later he recalled: "Well do I remember as in unreserved consecration I put myself, my life, my friends, my all upon the altar. I felt I was in the presence of God, entering into covenant with the Almighty."

With that commitment, Hudson Taylor set his face toward China and obscurity. He served Me well there and today is honored as the pioneer missionary to that country. And the other son, the one who wanted to make a name for himself, most people just remember him as Hudson Taylor's brother.

How can you serve Me better? Do what Mary did. Be sincere and give Me all you are and have. I'll take care of the rest.

Notes

1. Psalm 24:3–4.

2. Psalm 69:30–31.

3. Romans 8:6–8.

4. 1 Thessalonians 4:1–2.

5. 1 Thessalonians 1 is replete with those things that please God. Paul mentions their faithful work (v. 3), their labors prompted by love (v. 3), their enduring hope in the Lord Jesus (v. 3), their acceptance of the gospel message as coming from the Holy Spirit with power (v. 5), their deep conviction about the gospel message (v. 5), their willingness to imitate the Lord in their lives (v. 6), their joy in the face of severe suffering (v. 6), the model they were to other believers in how to live pleasing before the Lord (v. 7), their transmission of the gospel message to their communities (v. 8), their refusal to worship idols but turning to the true God instead (v. 9), and their patient waiting for the return of the Lord (v. 10).

6. Galatians 1:10.

7. Proverbs 16:7.

8. In the gospel of Matthew, Jesus had something to say about the kingdom in every chapter but three (14, 15, and 17) between the temptation near the beginning of His ministry and Gethsemane near the end.

9. Matthew 4:17; 16:28.

10. Acts 1:6–7.

11. Jesus said, "No one knows about that day or hour, not even the angels in heaven, nor the Son, but only the Father" (Mark 13:32). When the Son was on earth in the flesh, He voluntarily subjected Himself to servanthood and subordination to the Father; among His limitations was ignorance of the hour when He would return again to judgment. We need not worry about the time of His coming, but instead we are to do God's work and help others know Him better until that time.

12. Mark 13:33. Jesus often reiterated this need for readiness in His parables. That was the point of the parable about the men waiting for their master to return from a wedding banquet. The master didn't want to return to find them goofing off; he wanted them to greet his return with honest and energetic labor (Luke 12:35–40). "You also must be ready, because the Son of Man will come at an hour when you do not expect him." A similar message is taught in the parable of the ten virgins (Matthew 25:1–13). "Therefore keep watch, because you do not know the day or the hour."

13. 1 John 3:2–3.

14. Ezekiel 37, the vision of the valley of the dry bones is a prime example of this kind of prophecy.

15. In Matthew 24, Jesus mentioned that when the twigs of the fig tree begin to put forth their leaves, that is a harbinger of summer. So, too, the budding of the nation Israel would be a harbinger of Jesus' return to crush Satan's rebellion. It is important to remember, however, that while many of the signs in this passage have occurred, Jesus said "all these things" (Matthew 24:33) must come together at once to be a genuine indication that Jesus' return is imminent, and that has never yet been the case. However, after His return for His church, these things will fall into place like dominoes.

16. Daniel 8:23–25; 2 Thessalonians 2:9.

17. Daniel 9:27; Luke 21:20. He will invade the temple sanctuary and proclaim himself as the object of worship (Matthew 24:15; 2 Thessalonians 2:3–4). Then, stopping the daily sacrifice, he will erect an image of himself and require the Jews to worship him and his image (Daniel 8:11; 9:27; Revelation 13:14–15). Finally, he will destroy the temple (Daniel 8:11–14) and make Jerusalem desolate (Daniel 9:26b; Matthew 23:38–24:2), killing many Jews and leading others captive (Daniel 11:31–34; Isaiah 1:9; Jeremiah 30:7; Zechariah 13:8; Matthew 24:21; Luke 21:21–24).

18. John 14:2–3.

19. Malachi 1:8.

20. 2 Corinthians 9:6.

Miscellaneous

BARNA PROFILE

A variety of miscellaneous questions were asked by 4 percent of adults. Topics in this category were usually only brought up by one respondent. Typical questions with more than a single mention included:

1) Where are You?

2) Why do You make me so happy?

3) Why do You love us so much when we are so disobedient?

4) I have no questions for God.

YOUR QUESTION

1) Where are You?

GOD'S ANSWER

Most people ask *if* I exist, but not you. You want to know where I am and what I am doing when things don't seem to be right. Many times you wonder more about My silence than My location.

I know all things. I know how you can live forever. I know what will happen tomorrow. Listen, I knew on September 10, 2001, what would happen the next day. You wonder why I don't stop certain things from happening. Many have asked where I was on 9/11/2001.

Often I do intervene, though there is no way that you would know. No one showed up at choir practice one Wednesday night at West Side Baptist Church in Beatrice, Nebraska. These people were never late. But this Wednesday, at 7:30 P.M., none of them were at the church. Marilyn, the church pianist, overslept, so she and her mother were late. One high school sophomore was having trouble with her homework. One couple couldn't get their car started so they were unable to go and pick up other members. In fact, silently and unnoticed, I intervened in the lives of all eighteen choir members. At 7:30 P.M. there wasn't a soul in the church. And it's a good thing too, because there was a gas leak in the basement and precisely when the choir should have been practicing, a spark ignited the leak. The whole church burst into flames. Had you known how I worked in this situation, it would be evident that I don't have a "hands-off" policy when it comes to My creation.

But what about all those times I don't intervene and bad things happen? When Joni Eareckson was injured in a diving accident in 1967, I was there. I could have stopped it. But I didn't intervene. She became a quadriplegic, confined to a wheelchair, unable to use her hands. But I knew I would make something beautiful of her life. She learned to paint holding a brush in her teeth, and soon her works were prize collectors' items. I opened doors for her to write and in 1979 she founded Joni and Friends, a profound ministry to disabled people and their families. I had something better in mind for Joni. Through her ministry thousands of disabled people are blessed.

Where am I? Why don't I intervene in the troubles of the world? Sometimes I do and you don't recognize it, but sometimes I don't because I have knowledge you don't possess. My servant Isaiah was right about Me. "I make known the end from the beginning, from ancient times, what is still to come. I say: My purpose will stand, and I will do all that I please."[1]

Life is like a train. There is an engine and many boxcars. Your life is like one of those boxcars. You've lived in it for as long as you can remember. You've explored every nook and cranny of that car. You've discovered the best places to be if you want the smoothest ride. You've rumbled through life peeking through the boards on the sides of the car. There are a lot of unexplained things going on outside, but you have to settle for glimpses of them; you really don't understand them. You are headed down the tracks with some boxcars in front and others behind you. Those iron rails are unceasing influences on where you're going. And you don't even know where you are going. You live in a boxcar. You're not in front with the engine. You can't see where the track goes ahead of you. The walls of that boxcar bind your whole life.

But what if you were the engineer? What if you knew exactly where the tracks were and where they lead because you laid them? What if you were aware that after a steep, uphill climb there was a pleasant valley to follow?

Where am I? In the engine of the train. I'm the engineer. Why don't I always intervene with the troubles of the world? Because that state of your boxcar at any given moment is one connected to others, moving toward destinations unforeseen by you. You don't know how I will work for good in even the troubles and hardships you and others face. What you view as trouble today, you may come to be thankful for tomorrow. It all depends on how much you trust Me to know what I'm doing in the front of the train. Remember the words of King Solomon: "Trust in the LORD with all your heart and lean not on your own understanding; in all your ways acknowledge him, and he will make your paths straight."[2]

Where am I? I'm right where you need Me most—in front leading you and with you at all times. Let these words from the prophet Habakkuk reassure you and bring you peace. "The LORD is in his holy temple; let all the earth be silent before him."[3] I'm here for you.

YOUR QUESTION

2) Why do You make me so happy?

GOD'S ANSWER

Do you know what it means to be truly happy, according to Me? Happiness is not a mere feeling of giddiness, joviality, or cheerfulness. It's not just being in good spirits.

Biblical happiness knows that there must be more, because happiness in this life is so fleeting. One of your own writers, C. S. Lewis, said, "If I find in myself a desire which no experience in this world can satisfy, the most probable explanation is that I was made for another world."[4]

Happiness that is from Me is the expression of a transformed mind, a mind that is not constrained by present reality or squeezed into the world's mold.[5] Biblical happiness transcends things, people, places, events. It finds itself complete only when inextricably linked with Me. Christians are happy because they enjoy an intimate relationship with their Creator.[6]

So why do I make you happy? I made you for Myself and when you discovered Me, you discovered true happiness. I remind you how often My Word, the Bible, links your happiness to Me. The words "happy" and "blessed" are the same in the Old Testament, so those who find the greatest happiness are those who recognize the greatest blessings come from their relationship with Me.[7]

> "Blessed are you, O Israel! Who is like you, a people saved by the LORD? He is your shield and helper and your glorious sword." (Deuteronomy 33:29)
> "Blessed are all who fear the LORD, who walk in his ways." (Psalm 128:1)
> "Blessed are the people whose God is the LORD." (Psalm 144:15)

"Whoever gives heed to instruction prospers, and blessed is he who trusts in the LORD*."* (Proverbs 16:20)

"He who conceals his sins does not prosper, but whoever confesses and renounces them finds mercy. Blessed is the man who always fears the LORD*, but he who hardens his heart falls into trouble."* (Proverbs 28:13–14)

In the New Testament the concepts of happiness and blessedness are also the same. But for these believers, persecuted by the Romans and Jewish religious leaders alike, happiness took on a new quality—grace under fire. Jesus said, "I have set you an example that you should do as I have done for you. Now that you know these things, you will be blessed (happy) if you do them."[8] James was comforting persecuted believers when he said, "Brothers, as an example of patience in the face of suffering, take the prophets who spoke in the name of the Lord. As you know, we consider blessed those who have persevered."[9] And Peter agreed. Happiness consists both in a right relationship with Me and in rightly relating My way to the world. "But even if you should suffer for what is right, you are blessed."[10] And, "If you are insulted because of the name of Christ, you are blessed, for the Spirit of glory and of God rests on you."[11]

There is joy in getting close to Me that people who deny My existence will never know. Your happiness comes from the discovery that intimacy with the Almighty translates into loving service to others. That's why My Son, in what is called the Beatitudes, identified eight qualities of the blessed and happy.

1. *Blessed are the poor in spirit, for theirs is the kingdom of heaven.*

2. *Blessed are those who mourn, for they will be comforted.*

3. *Blessed are the meek, for they will inherit the earth.*

4. *Blessed are those who hunger and thirst for righteousness, for they will be filled.*

5. *Blessed are the merciful, for they will be shown mercy.*

6. *Blessed are the pure in heart, for they will see God.*

7. *Blessed are the peacemakers, for they will be called sons of God.*

8. *Blessed are those who are persecuted because of righteousness, for theirs is the kingdom of heaven.*[12]

Not many people are looking for happiness in mourning, meekness, or being merciful. But these lead to true happiness. And the happiest a person will ever be is in heaven. "No eye has seen, no ear has heard, no mind has conceived what God has prepared for those who love him."[13] Why are you so happy? You are picking up on the truth that there is more to the universe than material things.

YOUR QUESTION

3) Why do You love us so much when we are so disobedient?

GOD'S ANSWER

I have a question for you. Why are you so disobedient? Why do human lives always seem to be in trouble?

It is not human nature to do what is right; it is human nature to do what is wrong. Did you have to teach your children how to lie? No. They became experts with no one to coach them. Did you have to teach them to be jealous of their siblings, to want to take the things that belong to their brothers or sisters? No, they came by that naturally. Why? Human nature. As you know, humanity has a problem. In the Bible I call it sin, disobedience, and lawlessness. It affects all your relatives, all your friends, all your acquaintances, and all the people whom you don't know. It is universal and it is devastating.[14] "There is a way that seems right to a man, but in the end it leads to death."[15] You know that well. You are disobedient because you choose to be disobedient, and you choose to be disobedient because that's the inclination of your sinful nature.

But that's not My nature. My nature is to be holy, just, and loving.[16] My Book often speaks of My love. Paul the apostle said, "For I am convinced that neither death nor life, neither angels nor demons, neither the present nor the future, nor any powers, neither height nor depth, nor anything else in all creation, will be able to separate us from the love of God that is in Christ Jesus our Lord."[17] Paul also said, "When the kindness and love of God our Savior appeared, he saved us, not because of righteous things we had done, but because of his mercy."[18]

John the apostle agreed. "How great is the love the Father has lavished on us, that we should be called children of God . . . Whoever does not love does not know God, because God is love. This is how God showed his love among us: He sent his one and only Son into the world that we might live through him. This is love: not that we loved God, but that he loved us and sent his Son as an atoning sacrifice for our sins."[19]

You asked why I love you so much when you are so disobedient. Because that's who I am. I don't love your disobedience, but love is My nature, and I interact with you based on My nature, as you interact with others based on your nature.

Can you handle honesty? I don't love you because you are lovable; I love you because I am love. I told My people Israel, "I have loved you with an everlasting love: I have drawn you with loving-kindness."[20] They were not very lovable in the way they often treated Me. Even still, I not only told them of My love, but I also demonstrated it. I judged their sin because I am holy, but I forgave them when they repented, because I am love. I do the same with you. "You see, at just the right time, when we were still powerless, Christ died for the ungodly. Very rarely will anyone die for a righteous man, though for a good man someone might possibly dare to die. But God demonstrates his own love for us in this: While we were still sinners, Christ died for us."[21]

I have demonstrated My love for you in many ways, but chiefly when I sent My Son to be your Savior. Why did I love you when you were disobedient? Because I would save you from that disobedience and guide you to become the person you were created to be.

YOUR QUESTION

4) I have no questions for God.

GOD'S ANSWER

Most people don't know Me very well. Some people don't even believe in Me, let alone believe that I have the answers to their questions.[22] On the other end of the spectrum, there are people who say, "I already have the answers to my questions." That may sound arrogant to you, but these people have faith in Me and know they can find answers to their questions in My Word.

Many take the middle road, thinking that asking questions of God is for priests and pastors, theologians and philosophers, saying, "It is not my place to question God." They appeal to the sentiment of Isaiah 29:16 and Romans 9:20, which say the thing created has no right to question its Creator. And a few say, "You can't talk to God." Though they have questions and believe that I have the answers, they don't think they can connect with Me.

They have not discovered the ways that I have reached out to humanity through My Son, My Word, and My presence. But people who are familiar with Me know Me as a God of questions and answers. When a person reads the Bible consistently, questions jump off every page. Communicate with Me through prayer and I will answer.

When you have faith and trust in Me, you have a center in your life that makes sense. As Augustine said of Me, "Thou has made us for Thyself and we find no rest until we find rest in Thee." If you ask questions and seek answers in My Word, you'll find more than answers. You'll find Me and that will make all the difference in your life.

Notes

1. Isaiah 46:10.

2. Proverbs 3:5–6.

3. Habakkuk 2:20.

4. C. S. Lewis, *Mere Christianity* (New York: Collier, 1960), 106.

5. Romans 12:1–2.

6. Again, C. S. Lewis writes: "God designed the human machine to run on Himself. He Himself is the fuel our spirits were designed to burn, or the food our spirits were designed to feed on. There is no other. That is why it is just no good asking God to make us happy in our own way without bothering about religion. God cannot give us a happiness and peace apart from Himself, because it is not there. There is no such thing." *Mere Christianity*, 39.

7. Hebrew: *'esher.*

8. John 13:15, 17.

9. James 5:10–11.

10. 1 Peter 3:14.

11. 1 Peter 4:14.

12. Matthew 5:3–10.

13. 1 Corinthians 2:9.

14. Ezekiel 18:4; Romans 3:10, 23.

15. Proverbs 14:12.

16. Leviticus 20:7; Deuteronomy 32:4; Zephaniah 3:5; 1 Peter 1:16; 1 John 1:9; Revelation 15:3.

17. Romans 8:38–39.

18. Titus 3:4–5.

19. 1 John 3:1; 4:8–10, 16.

20. Jeremiah 31:3.

21. Romans 5:6–8.

22. The Pew survey in November of 2001 found that the largest single increase of any religious-related group was among those who professed no religion. In 1990 this category represented 14.3 million Americans (or about 8 percent of the population). In a decade the figure had doubled to 29.4 million (14.1 percent of the population). "Number of Americans with No Formal Religion Increasing, Survey Finds," by Chris Herlinger, *Christianity Today*, 7 January 2002. See online at: http://www.christianitytoday.com/ct/2002/100/33.0.html.

Author's Epilogue

As Joseph Heller wrote in his novel *Catch-22,* "Good God, how much reverence can you have for a Supreme Being who finds it necessary to include tooth decay in His divine system of creation?"[1] As you notice from this remark, the concept of divine responsibility for all the ills of this world is pervasive. Intended or not, most of the questions asked of God portrayed this underlying belief. But God didn't include tooth decay in His divine system of creation. His answers make that abundantly clear. If you wish to ask questions of God, you must be willing to let Him answer for Himself. When God does, His answers will not match your expectations.

Questions asked and answered. What now? Now you will filter God's answers through your experiences. You bring your own set of values to the questions asked of God. You view His responses through your presuppositions. You accept or reject His answers based upon your worldview. That way of seeing things may hinder your positive reception of God's answers. When that happens, you are faced with a critical decision. Whom do you trust? Are you willing to consider that God may be telling you what you don't want to hear, or do you simply dismiss His answer because of your predispositions? God has given honest answers; be equally honest in considering them.

Often Job is mentioned as one who had many questions for God. He put God at the center of his life. He feared God and shunned evil.[2] And yet, the bottom fell out of his life. Still, "in all this, Job did not sin by charging God with wrongdoing."[3] So, when Job asked God questions about why his life was so messed up, God answered his questions, right? Wrong. Job may have filtered God's answers through his worldview and likely accepted them, but God didn't even offer a response. He didn't reveal His master plan. Instead, He did something better: He revealed Himself. When Job's world was shaken to its very core and he encountered God in more than an intellectual way, his questions were not answered; they simply disappeared.[4]

If you did not get the answers you wanted from God, would you be willing to accept something better? In exchange for answers, will you accept encountering God in more than just an intellectual way? Madame Jeanne Guyon remarked, "If knowing answers to life's questions is absolutely necessary to you, then forget the journey. You will never make it, for this is a journey of unknowables—of unanswered questions, enigmas, incomprehensibles, and most of all, things unfair."[5] There is something better than answers—there is God.

Regardless of what presuppositions you brought with your questions, let God speak for Himself. Give Him a chance to reveal Himself to you. Go back to the footnotes at the end of each chapter, look up the references in your Bible, and read in God's own words what He has to say. When you do, set aside your preconceived notions of what His answers should be, and what you find will be much more valuable than answers. You will discover God Himself.

Notes

1. Joseph Heller, *Catch-22* (New York: Del, 1989), 176.

2. Job 1:1.

3. Job 1:22.

4. Job 38–42.

5. Madame Jeanne Guyon, *Spiritual Torrents* (Augusta, Maine: Christian Books, 1984), 48.

How the Barna Poll Was Conducted

THE QUESTION AND RESPONSES

The purpose of the poll was to identify the questions that Americans would ask of God if they had the opportunity. The graph on the next page indicates by response the most popular topics.

The question was open-ended and qualitative in nature. To analyze these responses, all questions asked by the respondents were recorded verbatim. Each individual response was read, and then coding categories were developed to reflect the common themes or topics that emerged. Responses were then recoded into the appropriate topical category.

Data from this study was also analyzed by relevant segments or subgroups. This type of analysis enables a

TOPIC OF SINGLE MOST IMPORTANT
QUESTION TO ASK GOD ABOUT LIFE
(% response)

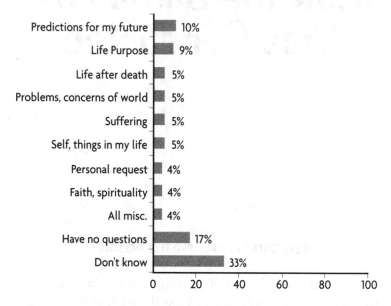

glimpse at the characteristics or behaviors of particular groups of interest. All differences within categories described here are statistically significant at the 95 percent confidence level.

RESEARCH DEFINITIONS

Faith Segments

Born Again: The term *"born-again Christian"* does *not* come from people referring to themselves by this label. Barna Research surveys include two questions regarding beliefs that are used to classify people as born again or not born again. To be classified as a born-again Christian, individuals must say they have made a personal commitment to Jesus Christ that is still important in their life today, and that after they die they will go to heaven because they have confessed their sins and accepted Jesus Christ as their Savior. People who meet these criteria are classified as born again regardless of whether or not they would say they are born-again Christians.

Evangelical: The term *"evangelical"* is applied to born-again Christians who also meet seven additional criteria. Those include: (1) saying their faith is very important in their life, (2) believing they have a responsibility to share their faith in Christ with non-Christians, (3) believing in the existence of Satan, (4) believing that eternal salvation is gained through God's grace alone, not through our efforts, (5) believing that Jesus Christ lived a sinless life, (6) believing the Bible is accurate in all that it teaches, and (7) choosing an orthodox definition of God. This definition has no relationship to church attendance, membership, or denominational affiliation.

Notional: The term *"notional"* Christian is applied to those who consider themselves to be Christian but either do not have a personal commitment to Jesus Christ or do not believe that they will experience eternal favor with God based solely on His grace and mercy.

Denominational Affiliation

Mainline Attenders: Self-identify as attending a church of one of the following denominations: United Church of Christ, Episcopal, Lutheran, Methodist, or Presbyterian.

NonMainline Attenders: Self-identify as attending a Christian church other than a mainline denomination. This category includes those attending Adventist, AME/African Methodist Episcopal, Assembly of God, Baptist, Christian, Church of God, Disciples of Christ, Evangelical, Mennonite, Nazarene, Orthodox, Pentecostal, Reformed, Wesleyan, Brethren, Holiness, or nondenominational/independent.

All Protestants: Self-identify as attending a Christian church, excluding: Catholic, Jehovah's Witness, Mormon/ Latter Day Saints, Orthodox, Jewish, atheist/agnostic, Muslim, Buddhist, and Hindu.

Catholics: Self-identify as attending a Catholic church.

Generations

Busters: those born between 1966 and 1985.

Boomers: those born between 1965 and 1946.

Elders: those born before 1946.

METHODOLOGY

The poll included 1,010 telephone interviews conducted among a representative sample of adults over the age of eighteen within the forty-eight continental United States. The survey was conducted from January 17–February 4, 2003. All interviews were conducted from the Barna Research Group (BRG) telephone center in Ventura, California. The sampling error for this poll is plus or minus three percentage points, at the 95 percent confidence level.

The survey calls were made at various times during the day and evening. If an individual did not answer, at least four more attempts were made at different times of the day, in order to maximize the possibility of contact. This is a quality control procedure that ensures individuals in the sampling frame have an equivalent probability of inclusion within the survey, thereby increasing the survey reliability.

The average interview lasted sixteen minutes. Experienced, trained interviewers conducted all of the interviews. They were supervised at all times, and every interviewer was monitored using the Silent Monitoring™ system employed by the Barna Research Group.

The survey was conducted through the use of the CATI (Computer Assisted Telephone Interviewing) system in place at the BRG field center. This process ensures that interviewers properly administer question-skip patterns and that survey data are recorded accurately.

Based upon U.S. Census data sources, regional and ethnic quotas were designed to ensure that the final group of adults interviewed reflected the distribution of adults nationwide and adequately represented the three primary ethnic groups within the United States (identified by Barna Research Group as Whites, Blacks, and Hispanics). The final survey data was balanced according to gender.

In this study, the cooperation rate among participants was 87 percent. This is an unusually high rate (i.e., the industry norm is about 60 percent), and it significantly raises the confidence we may place in the resulting statistics. In every survey there are a variety of ways in which the accuracy of the data can be affected. The lower the cooperation rate, the less representative the respondents interviewed may be of the population from which they were drawn, thereby reducing the accuracy of the results. Other sources of potential error include: question-design bias, question-order bias, interviewer mistakes, sampling error, and respondent deception. Many of these types of errors cannot be accurately estimated. However, having a high cooperation rate does enhance the reliability of the information procured.

SINCE 1894, Moody Publishers has been dedicated to equip and motivate people to advance the cause of Christ by publishing evangelical Christian literature and other media for all ages, around the world. Because we are a ministry of the Moody Bible Institute of Chicago, a portion of the proceeds from the sale of this book go to train the next generation of Christian leaders.

If we may serve you in any way in your spiritual journey toward understanding Christ and the Christian life, please contact us at www.moodypublishers.com.

"All Scripture is God-breathed and is useful for teaching, rebuking, correcting and training in righteousness, so that the man of God may be thoroughly equipped for every good work."
—2 TIMOTHY 3:16, 17

MOODY
PUBLISHERS

THE NAME YOU CAN TRUST®

AN INTERVIEW WITH GOD TEAM

ACQUIRING EDITOR
Mark Tobey

COPY EDITOR
Ali Childers

BACK COVER COPY
Anne Perdicaris

COVER DESIGN
Paetzold Associates

INTERIOR DESIGN
Ragont Design

PRINTING AND BINDING
Dickinson Press Inc.

The typeface for the text of this book is
Sabon